The Scientific Measurement
of International Conflict

D1563529

The Scientific Measurement of International Conflict

□ □ □ □ □ □ □ □ □ □ □ □ □ □ □ □ □ □

Handbook of Datasets on Crises and Wars, 1495–1988 A.D.

Claudio Cioffi-Revilla

Lynne Rienner Publishers □ Boulder & London

Dedicated to the mission of the
United Nations Office for Research and
the Collection of Information

Published in the United States of America in 1990 by
Lynne Rienner Publishers, Inc.
1800 30th Street, Boulder, Colorado 80301

and in the United Kingdom by
Lynne Rienner Publishers, Inc.
3 Henrietta Street, Covent Garden, London WC2E 8LU

Library of Congress Cataloging-in-Publication Data
Cioffi-Revilla, Claudio A., 1951-
  The scientific measurement of international conflict:
handbook of datasets on crises and wars, 1495-1988 A.D./
Claudio Cioffi-Revilla
  Includes bibliographical references
  ISBN 1-55587-194-1 (alk. paper)
  1. International relations—Research. 2. War—Research.
I. Title.
JX1291.C483   1989   89-39491
327.1'6'0287—dc20   CIP

British Cataloguing in Publication Data
A Cataloguing in Publication record for this book
is available from the British Library.

Printed and bound in the United States of America

The paper used in this publication meets the requirements
of the American National Standard for Permanence of
paper for Printed Library Materials Z39.48-1984.

Contents

v

Tables and Figures

Preface

Earth and space scientists—astronomers, meteorologists, seismologists, volcanologists—place great emphasis on the study of severe phenomena in their fields; the scientific measurement of physical events such as solar flares, sunspots, hurricanes, earthquakes, and volcanic eruptions is high on their research agendas. Consequently, the systematic, reliable measurement of these phenomena occupies a great deal of scientific attention and resources. In the United States, the National Science Foundation (NSF) has an entire division specifically dedicated to measurement and instrumentation, and the National Institute of Standards and Technology (formerly the National Bureau of Standards) also plays a prominent role in this area.

During the last few decades a similar emphasis on measurement has developed in the social sciences, aimed at significantly improving our basic scientific understanding of and capacity to predict severe social phenomena. In the social universe, severe phenomena typically involve the violent deaths of groups of human beings, or the destruction of their wealth and resources. Well-known examples of such events include economic depressions, violent strikes, revolutions, acts of terrorism, and wars.

This book is about some of the highest quality scientific information presently available—in terms that are accessible to virtually anyone in the scientific community—concerning the incidence, magnitude, extent, and other empirical dimensions of conflict behavior between nations. The primary focus is on international crises and wars because these are the main forms of severe, deadly international conflicts. The time period (historical timeline) covered by the book is the last 500 years, from the late fifteenth century to the late twentieth century. In comparative terms, five centuries of data in *any* field of empirical science represent a highly valuable asset on which to build theory. Certainly, Tycho Brahe never provided *that* many data to Johannes Kepler!

Crises and wars in the international system are clearly a matter of great concern to many civilized individuals worldwide, including physical scientists who write on war and peace as an avocation.[1] The actual scientific work involved in this field of social science is difficult and highly specialized. When poorly done, the resulting data are scientifically worthless. Thus, work in this area requires training similar to that required of researchers in the earth and space sciences for conducting accurate, reliable measurements of severe phenomena occurring in complex systems. The measurement of international conflict discussed in this book is done by a number of contemporary political scientists and their research associates, working in some of the leading university research projects in the United States under the auspices of a set of funding agencies, including the NSF. The projects that are documented and compared here are by no means the only ones in existence, but they are among the most scientifically accurate, reliable, and potentially valuable for advancing our basic scientific understanding of war and peace patterns over the past five centuries.

This book contains three chapters. The first chapter introduces the topic of measuring international conflict in general—as a recordable form of empirical social behavior—and provides background for the specific datasets that are the focus of this book. Also included in this chapter is some context for understanding the nature and purpose of NSF's Data Development for International Relations (DDIR) Project, though no attempt has been made to provide a detailed historical account. The second chapter contains the rationale for and description of the standard of information developed in this study—the ICDC (Interstate Conflict Datasets Catalog) standard. This standard is then used to describe in detail each of the eight DDIR interstate conflict datasets (four datasets on crises and four on wars). The main reference material (the information profile of each dataset) is included in Chapter 2. The third chapter presents preliminary comparisons of the eight datasets, focusing on a set of important dimensions: distribution, space-time coverage, parameter estimates (e.g., aggregate onset rates), conceptualizations of conflict events, and sources of information employed by the datasets. Some of the methods employed in this comparative analysis, such as logic event analysis for comparing conflict events, are new, whereas other methods, such as probabilistic models for the onset of crises and wars, are extensions of well-established methods. Most of the material included in this last chapter should be viewed as exploratory, as it is only recently that a sufficient variety

---

[1] To use a physicist's own expression: "It has been interesting to discover how many of the early physical scientists observed and wrote about social phenomena as a hobby" [Elliot W. Montroll and Wade W. Badger (1974), *Introduction to Quantitative Aspects of Social Phenomena* (New York: Gordon and Breach Science Publishers), p. v]. The founder of quantitative international relations, as well as modern peace research as an empirical and mathematical science, was the late British physicist and meteorologist Lewis Fry Richardson (F.R.S.).

of datasets exists to allow comparative analysis. A combined bibliography of all references is listed at the end of the book.

A brief account of how this book originated will provide a broader substantive and scientific context than its specialized subject matter would tend to suggest. I began to write the book some four years ago, while at the University of Illinois at Urbana-Champaign, initially intending it only for my personal use in connection with research and teaching. As a mathematical modeler of international conflict and peace processes—and not unlike many others in this area—I basically wanted to have a precise, comprehensive idea of the existing datasets available to empirically fit and test the probability models I was developing. Although I was aware of these datasets, and in fact had already used a few of them, I lacked the broad, detailed knowledge that I deemed necessary for making sound judgments and practical choices.

Three things puzzled me as I began to gather the information I needed to develop an inventory of the conflict datasets compiled in various countries. First, in spite of the fact that the discipline of international relations had already spent several decades of very hard work in this area, the field as a whole lacked a comprehensive survey of existing datasets. My second puzzle was that, aside from the information contained in some dataset "codebooks," or in a handful of general references scattered in the literature, no one seemed to possess detailed information that was also comprehensive in scope. I also recall that about the same time there was a great deal of heated discussion about the status of "scientific cumulation" (or the lack thereof) in international relations. At that point I realized that not only my own research program, but those of others as well, might benefit from having a good scientific inventory available. Finally, and perhaps most surprisingly, although virtually every one of the dataset collectors I talked to about the desirability of putting together a truly comprehensive study of datasets seemed enthusiastic about the idea, no one seemed willing to do it. Not being a data collector myself—but a mathematical modeler, a *user* of datasets—I had naively assumed that someone in the area of data collection (or elsewhere in the discipline for that matter) had at some time in the not-too-distant past undertaken the important task of putting together a reasonably comprehensive survey of existing datasets, perhaps in order to determine which data to collect and which not to collect. It occurred to me that, if nothing else, an inventory could help avoid some otherwise likely replication of effort and build upon previously successful methods. Perhaps even more important, it seemed to me that thorough, comprehensive studies are a basic scientific requirement prior to having exciting discussions about the cumulation of knowledge in any field.

In 1984, about two years after I had begun my international survey of existing conflict datasets, the DDIR Project of the NSF (described later, in

Chapter 1) began to take shape under the coordination of Richard L. Merritt and Dina A. Zinnes, colleagues at the Merriam Lab.[2]   Although the international archive of datasets on which I was working was much broader in scope than the DDIR Project (which is limited to some of the major U.S.-based projects), I agreed to develop that portion of my archive pertaining to the six DDIR data projects on interstate conflict under the aegis of the DDIR initiative in what eventually became DDIR Project 6 (the Interstate Conflict Datasets Catalog).

I finished this book in 1989, after leaving the University of Illinois to begin a new and exciting research program at the University of Colorado at Boulder involving both mathematical modeling and data collection—the Long-Range Analysis of War (LORANOW) project.[3] I decided to publish this book on DDIR datasets, and not wait until the more comprehensive LORANOW study is completed, because a number of colleagues and students have encouraged me to do so, suggesting that it could provide a useful reference worth disseminating. Pragmatism aside, I am also happy to publish it because the datasets that constitute the core of this book are a product of love, hard labor, and dedication to the pursuit of knowledge. Their existence and high scientific value must not go unpublicized.   The international research community will recognize this, hopefully, and profit from the vast amount and high quality of information they contain. In particular, those of us engaged in mathematical modeling benefit from the existence of these modern empirical archives—they permit our models to address the real world of conflict and peace among nations, making mathematical theories more scientifically valuable, perhaps even relevant, to global public policy on matters of international security.

---

[2]In 1984, Patrick J. McGowan (Department of Political Science, Arizona State University) conducted a survey of datasets used by U.S. scholars in quantitative international politics, known as the McGowan Report. [See Patrick J. McGowan (1984), Report of a Survey of International Relations Scholars on Significant Datasets, Tempe: Arizona State University, Department of Political Science, 14 June, mimeo.]   A version of the earlier survey was later published as Patrick J. McGowan (1986), Data Priorities in International Research: Views of North American International and Comparative Politics Researchers, *DDIR-UPDATE: Newsletter of the N.S.F. DDIR Project* 1(2: Appendix) December 1986: A1-A3. The McGowan Report was a cornerstone to what later became the DDIR Project, because it was instrumental in providing the community of scholars with factual information about data utilization.

[3]For information on the LORANOW project, write to: Claudio Cioffi-Revilla, LORANOW Project, Center for International Relations, Campus Box 333, University of Colorado, Boulder, CO 80309-0333.; or electronic mail by Bitnet/Internet: CIOFFI_C@CUBLDR.COLORADO.EDU

The book is addressed to all those with an interest in world affairs and empirical, real-world traits of war and peace—readers ranging from students and academic researchers to security analysts and other public officials in private or public institutions. Because international conflict and peace studies constitute an interdisciplinary area, the book will be useful to colleagues in a number of academic disciplines, such as history, political science, sociology, economics, applied mathematical modeling, statistics, public policy analysis, and—not least of all—peace research (or peace science) and conflict studies. Many researchers in these and other disciplines have already used several datasets discussed in this book.

The book is also a source of real-world information (very real, indeed) for international security and other global risk analysts, as well as for policy officials, whether in private or public institutions, who have an operational interest in and key political responsibility for trends and patterns in world affairs, particularly with regard to the very empirical phenomenon of war and peace among nations. The recent creation of an Office for Research and Collection of Information at the United Nations must be viewed as an encouraging, timely development. As I explain later in more detail, the information contained in this volume cannot easily (if at all) be found outside of scientific research circles. It directly concerns an international matter of the highest public and private priority. In this century alone wars of various magnitudes have been experienced by over a billion human beings in all regions of the planet. The total human population that has been directly affected by war in the course of recorded history (the total population at risk) cannot yet be easily estimated by reliable methods, but it is obviously of enormous magnitude. Thus, scientifically collected information about war is not at all a purely academic pursuit, although rigorous scientific study may be the only rational way to advance our rudimentary understanding of this ancient and destructive form of social behavior. From a security policy perspective, this book is therefore about the systematic assessment of an important dimension of collective human behavior, a type of violent behavior (war) that is prominent in our species. Information of this sort should be considered highly relevant by those charged with international security responsibilities—lest our species not survive "the human experiment."

Claudio Cioffi-Revilla

Acknowledgments

I wish to acknowledge the valuable assistance received from many colleagues and students in the preparation of this study. J. David Singer and his co-investigator, Paul R. Williamson, provided me with generous amounts of information concerning the largest dataset project of concern to this study—the Correlates of War project at the University of Michigan. Singer shared valuable advice as well as project-related bibliographic information that otherwise would have taken much longer to compile. Francis A. Beer, University of Colorado at Boulder, was an early enthusiastic supporter of this type of basic scientific reference documentation for our field, and, although his own conflict datasets are not documented in this compendium (Beer 1982, 1983a,b,c,d, 1984, 1989), I remain indebted for his interest and encouragement throughout. My colleagues in the Center for International Relations of the University of Colorado at Boulder, Steve Chan and Michael D. Ward, also provided me with useful comments, and I am grateful for their enthusiasm.

Final collection and preparation of the information contained in this book was made possible in part through support from the Data Development for International Relations (DDIR) Project of the U.S. National Science Foundation, under DDIR Sub-Project 6, the "Interstate War Catalog" (described in *DDIR-UPDATE* [the newsletter of the DDIR Project], 1 (1) October 1986: 3). Support during the last stages was provided by the University of Colorado at Boulder (in particular, the Center for International Relations, the Department of Political Science, and the College of Arts and Sciences). I am grateful to Pierangelo Isernia, Forum Humanum Project of the Club of Rome, for assisting me with various tasks of data collection and archiving during early stages of this study, in the spring semester of the academic year 1987/88, while I was still at the University of Illinois. Many thanks are also due to my research assistants in the LORANOW Project, Woondo Choi and Melanie Mason (University of Colorado at Boulder), and to Kun Y. Park (Texas A & M University) for many helpful comments and suggestions. I have also benefited from useful comments received at the 1989 Workshop of the Working Group on Supplemental Ways for Improving International Stability (WG SWIIS) of the International Federation for Automatic Control (IFAC), held in Budapest, Hungary, under the auspices of the Hungarian Academy of Sciences. My sincere thanks to Harold Chestnut (President, SWIIS Foundation), Peter Kopacek (Systems Research Institute, Johannes Kepler Universität, Linz, Austria) and Tibor Vamos (Computer and Automation Institute, Hungarian Academy of Sciences, Budapest) for their invitation to present a summary of this work at the IFAC/SWIIS workshop, and to the conference participants for their many helpful comments.

Clearly, this compendium could not have been completed—perhaps not even imagined—without the vital collaboration I received from the principal investigators of the eight datasets described herein: Charles S. Gochman (University of Pittsburgh), Jack S. Levy (Rutgers University), Manus I. Midlarsky (Rutgers University), Frederic S. Pearson (University of Missouri–St. Louis), J. David Singer (University of Michigan), and Jonathan Wilkenfeld (University of Maryland). To all of them, as well as to their project assistants, go my sincerest thanks and appreciation for the time devoted to sharing vital information and checking for accuracy and completeness. The scientific community is indebted to all of them. However, I alone am responsible for any errors that might remain.

Finally, a note of clarification: In this book the term "DDIR datasets" is used simply to refer to the eight datasets that constitute the main concern here. Although useful as a shorthand, the term is technically incorrect, and it may be seriously misleading if it suggests to the reader that the totality of the information contained in these datasets—or even the majority of it in the case of some datasets—owes its existence solely to the DDIR Project. It should be stressed that almost without exception these dataset projects have had (and many will continue to have) multiple sources of funding support, and this of course includes but is not limited to funding by the NSF. No single agency—certainly not the DDIR Project alone—could possibly have funded the collection and maintenance of all the valuable information described in this book. It is important to realize that, from the perspective of the principal investigators (though without claiming to speak on their behalf on this matter), the DDIR Project of the NSF is only one recent source of funding support, albeit a major one. To support projects such as these requires an endless, highly demanding, and often thankless effort on the part of the principal investigators and others. Universities, their departments and research institutes, together with private and public foundations are to be equally acknowledged for providing indispensable support, sometimes in intangible forms. Therefore, I ask the reader to remember that the term "DDIR datasets" is only a shorthand for a more complex and intricate research endeavor, one distributed over half a dozen universities and headed by principal investigators who have to constantly struggle to secure project funds while maintaining steady progress with high scientific standards. This book wishes to celebrate their pioneering success.

To my wife Jean go my *grazie infinite!* for her constant, intelligent, and cheerful encouragement over many years—during my bright moments, as well as in sadder ones, when tasks such as these seemed endless and hopeless. Without Jean and her music I could not have brought this study to completion.

Lynne Rienner and her hard-working staff, in particular Steve Barr, deserve credit for their enthusiasm, careful editing, and high standards.

Indeed, one might do well to begin the study of a system with pure description, devoid of theoretical considerations apart from the selection of indices, which is inadvertently influenced by preconceived ideas or commitments. . . .

One can go a step further by introducing the time dimension. A question that naturally suggests itself is whether the total amount of violence engendered by war has increased, decreased, or remained fairly constant in recent history. . . .

To look at the international system with somewhat greater resolving power, we turn to the use of indices describing so-called crises.

—ANATOL RAPOPORT, *Mathematical Models in the Social and Behavioral Sciences*

1
Introduction

This chapter describes historical and methodological antecedents, and some basic scientific assumptions, about measuring international conflict behavior. It also provides background information on the specific set of social science data collections described in the following chapters. The core information about each dataset—the set of information profiles—is reported in the next chapter (which may be read independently of this first chapter). However, the reader will benefit more by understanding several assumptions, scientific objectives, and limitations characteristic of these datasets.

1.1 Scientific Measurement of International Conflict Behavior

1.1.1 Scientific Motivation

Almost three decades ago, two great American pioneers in the application of mathematics to social science, John G. Kemeny and J. Laurie Snell, made the following important observation:

> The scientific method may initially be described as a cyclic process through which human beings learn from experience. As evidence accumulates, theories in better agreement with the actual functioning of nature can be formulated.[1]

Science—including the social science of international relations—is based on this dynamic interplay between theory and evidence. At about the same time, another great U.S. scientist, James S. Coleman, was even more explicit about the vital nexus that exists between mathematical theory (models) and empirical measurement. He discussed this as follows:

---

[1]John G. Kemeny and J. Laurie Snell (1962), *Mathematical Models in the Social Sciences* (Cambridge, Mass.: The MIT Press), p. 3.

What is it about quantitative measurement that is so crucial for theory-development? Essentially this: the power of a theory to provide precise and numerous deductions lies in its ability to carry out transformations—in fact, chains of transformations—upon the input data.

If these data are in the form of numbers, and maintain their properties as numbers after the transformations, then the powerful transformations of algebra, calculus, and matrix algebra can be carried out upon them. If the data do not obey these requirements, then these powerful tools are unusable. Thus the task of assigning numbers so that they meet these requirements is a crucial one for any science—and it is a task extremely difficult to meet in social science.[2]

Today, half a century after the first empirical efforts in the measurement of international conflict were pioneered by the British meteorologist Lewis Fry Richardson (1881–1953), the founder of modern, scientific peace and conflict research, the essential role of intersubjective, systematic, and reliable data about peace, conflicts, and war remains critical to social scientists, statisticians, and other analysts and scientists working in this area (Rapoport 1983: 429–464).

Indeed, the empirical observation and measurement of war and peace phenomena are as essential to the task of scientific research on interstate relations as worldwide weather data have become for other fields of empirical science, such as meteorology and climatology. Of course, even the best data are not single-handedly responsible for scientific progress—mathematical models are equally important for constructing theory by means of more formal approaches (these offer logical decidability). Further, because mathematical contributions to conflict and peace theory have increased in both quantity and quality, the potential uses of reliable data (analytical "transformations," as Coleman would say) have also increased. Thus, a field of empirical science—such as conflict and peace research have traditionally claimed to be—cannot develop far and fruitfully without frequent regard to its factual, empirical base. Measurement is as necessary as mathematical modeling, as noted almost a generation ago by Kemeny, Snell, and Coleman.

This book seeks to provide a comprehensive and reliable description, and offer some preliminary comparative analyses, of a set of major datasets now available to the scientific research community (including both social and physical scientists) on the hazardous phenomenon of international conflict. These are the interstate conflict datasets of the U.S. National Science Foundation's Project on Data Development for International Research

---

[2]James S. Coleman (1964), *Introduction to Mathematical Sociology* (New York: The Free Press of Glencoe), p. 56.

(DDIR). Although these are by no means the only datasets available in this particular field of social science (as we shall see in the next section), the DDIR datasets on interstate conflict are among the most reliable publicly available data collections on worldwide patterns of war and peace in history.

1.1.2   A Brief History of International Conflict Measurement

The scientific measurement of international conflicts as historical episodes or events (i.e., events under the general rubric of crises, armed interventions, and wars of various types and magnitudes) has a relatively young history in social science. The effort began earlier in this century, primarily through the pioneering work of three great scientists: Lewis F. Richardson (1960; a posthumous compilation of 1941, 1945a, 1945b, and other earlier works), Quincy Wright (1942), and Pitirim A. Sorokin (1937). These three scientists reported on the first projects ever attempted to scientifically record the incidence, magnitude, duration, and other observable descriptive characteristics of severe conflict between social groups or nations on a worldwide, longitudinal basis. Indeed, their originality stems from having involved—for the first time in the history of social science—the use of empirical, reliable counting criteria to record the conflict behavior of many social groups and nations over many years.

Since the 1930s and 1940s, dozens of other empirical data collection projects have developed, primarily at universities and research institutes in the United States and Western Europe. Among the better known of these projects are the Dimensionality of Nations (DON) project at the University of Hawaii (R. J. Rummel); the Stanford 1914 Crisis project (R. C. North); the University of Michigan's Correlates of War (COW) project (J. D. Singer and M. Small); MIT's Interstate Conflict Data project (H. Alker, Jr., R. L. Butterworth, and Frank L. Sherman); the Comparative Research on the Events of Nations (CREON) project at the Ohio State University (C. F. Hermann); the International Crisis Behavior (ICB) project at the University of Maryland (J. Wilkenfeld) and McGill University (M. Brecher); the World Events Interactions Survey (WEIS) at the University of Southern California (C. A. McClelland); and the Conflict and Peace Data Bank (COPDAB) project at the University of North Carolina until the early 1980s and at the University of Maryland since then (E. E. Azar). The datasets produced by these conflict and peace research projects over the years represent a remarkable U.S. national science resource (Starr 1987), available to the international scientific community everywhere.

Some other less well known empirical datasets on international conflict include the following: the new International and National Data on the European System (INDES) project at the Europa Institute of the

University of Amsterdam (J. Faber and R. Groenink); the Banca de Eventos Datos de America Latina (BADAL) project in Argentina and Venezuela (A. Cisneros-Lavaller); the University of Florence's Banca di Eventi Internazionali Europei (BEUR) project (U. Gori and F. Attinà); the Hungarian Academy of Sciences' Wars of Ten Years project (I. Kende); the Società Italiana per l'Organizzazione Internazionale's (SIOI) databases in Rome (F. A. Casadio); the Institut Français de Polémologie databases in Paris (G. Bouthoul and R. Carrere); and the new hypertext datasets of the Long-Range Analysis of War (LORANOW) project at the University of Colorado at Boulder (C. Cioffi-Revilla).[3]

Clearly, much of the methodology and the theoretical background involved in measuring international conflict has changed since the early days of Richardson, Wright, and Sorokin. For instance, different standards and methods have emerged, depending on the time-scale or frame of reference utilized to measure international events (events data vs. episodic data). This distinction often is referred to as fine vs. coarse data, depending on whether days or years are used as the basic unit of measurement. These and other research trends point toward an increased level of specialization in the measurement of international behavior, whether of a conflictual or of a cooperative nature. However, the central scientific mission of these projects has remained the same: to systematically observe and record the incidence of international conflict in history and across societies, using the most widely accepted scientific standards. Such standards consist of empirical operationalizations made public to members of the research community, intersubjective and reliable coding procedures, replicability of observations, documentation of sources used to create the dataset, and others. The scientific quality of datasets may differ, insofar as the rigorous implementation of these stringent canons may vary across datasets.

1.1.3   Existing Scientific Documentation

The empirical field of international conflict measurement is so new that its systematic scientific documentation—providing detailed information about existing datasets and their practical use—can at best be described as scattered

---

[3]These as well as many other conflict datasets (totalling approximately sixty) are currently being inventoried, surveyed, and assessed as part of the scientific documentation work being conducted at the LORANOW project at the University of Colorado at Boulder (Cioffi-Revilla 1989b). One result of this effort will be publication of the *International Handbook of Conflict Datasets* (*IHCD*), containing the information profile of all identified datasets in this area, once the information is sufficiently complete. Interested researchers may write to the author to obtain more information on the current status of the *IHCD*.

and ranging from incomplete to nonexistent. At present, most of the useful information concerning these datasets is contained in only two types of documentation sources, neither of which is practical for consultation purposes by analysts and other potential users.

The first type of available source consists of the actual codebook of a given dataset, assuming one actually exists. Often such documents are written in the beginning of the computer tape reel containing the dataset, so the tape must be obtained, mounted, and so on. In addition, for some datasets a potential user may refer to publications in the form of monographs or articles that have appeared in the specialized professional journals. Aside from these two documentation sources there are few other aids of reference that are easily accessible to researchers and students, and some of these are not that easy to access. Consequently, at present a full library of heterogeneous materials is required to understand the content and research potential of these datasets.

The most systematic survey with a fairly extensive coverage of some existing datasets is already half a decade old (Beer 1983a), and focuses primarily on the pioneer datasets of Richardson, Wright, and Sorokin, in addition to the more recent dataset collected in the Correlates of War project. Two other surveys are currently in preparation: one has specialized focus on datasets of many different types of social conflict and peace behavior (Cioffi-Revilla 1989c); the other covers a selection of international and comparative politics data, with less specialized emphasis on conflict and peace patterns (Merritt and Zinnes 1986). All in all, the present book is the only source providing homogeneous, comparative coverage of some of the principal datasets on international conflict.

1.1.4   Types of Conflict Measures

As with other social phenomena having a multidimensional character, the dimensions of international conflict are measurable with varying degrees of precision.   International conflict—more generally, social interaction— manifests both qualitative and quantitative aspects, as well as continuous and discrete properties. This aspect alone makes international conflict a complex phenomenon, aside from any other consideration based on the social dynamics of the phenomenon.

Following the so-called Stevens convention,[4] we may distinguish between nominal, ordinal, interval, and ratio (or cardinal) levels of

---

[4] S. S. Stevens (1951), "Mathematics, Measurement, and Psychophysics." In *Handbook of Experimental Psychology*, pp. 1-49 (New York: John Wiley & Sons).

measurement.   Although physical scientists use other distinctions for referring to levels of precision in their variables (they primarily distinguish between continuous and discrete scales), this four-type distinction is useful to social scientists because it places emphasis on a scale of precision that goes from qualitative (nominal) to quantitative (ratio) values of given variables.

The scientific measurement of international conflict is based primarily on nominal and ratio levels of precision, with some instances of ordinal measurement (e.g., for measuring the approximate intensity of war probability during crises as low, medium, or high).   Examples of nominal level measures of international conflict include types of conflicts, their geographic location, the identity of belligerents, and other taxonomic (qualitative) attributes of severe international interactions.   By contrast, many measures (variables) of conflict intensity assume ratio or cardinal values. Some examples of this more precise, fully quantitative set of dimensions are the following: fatality, either as a rate (fatalities/year) or as the total fatality count for the duration of a conflict; number of belligerent participants; and time durations.   The datasets described in the next chapter contain other examples.

Because international conflict is a multidimensional empirical phenomenon (like severe weather), taken together these measures help us describe patterns of onset, magnitude, duration, diffusion, and other key variables.   A large family of mathematical models already exists for using these rich datasets for model-building purposes to then draw testable deductions and predictions through analysis.   However, in part because of the documentation problems pointed out earlier, at present most of the scientific potential of these datasets remains largely unfulfilled.   The documentation of existing datasets is therefore a crucial step toward realizing that potential.

1.2   The U.S. National Science Foundation's Project on Data Development for International Research

1.2.1   Project Background

In 1986, the Political Science Program of the U.S. National Science Foundation approved an unprecedented three-year grant proposal to fund a nationwide scientific project in the social sciences entitled "Data Development for International Research."   Richard L. Merritt and Dina A. Zinnes (Merriam Laboratory for Analytic Political Research, University of Illinois at Urbana-Champaign) became coordinators for the umbrella DDIR Project.   Many other international relations scholars with an interest in data collection and analysis participated in this effort, in one capacity or another, as chronicled in various issues of the newsletter of the NSF DDIR Project, *DDIR-UPDATE*. By the spring of 1989, the DDIR Project had held numerous scientific meetings with many active researchers (and a few pioneers as well) in the joint international areas of peace research, conflict studies, and quantitative international politics.

The DDIR Project as a whole (i.e., the umbrella project funded by the NSF) encompassed two different scientific objectives with regard to international relations data collection and maintenance. (These are described in greater detail in *DDIR-UPDATE*, vol. 1, no. 1, October 1986, as well as in the original proposal submitted to and approved by the NSF). The first scientific objective of the DDIR Project consisted of active, ongoing financial support for a limited set of existing or new international data collection projects (the data are international, not the collection effort), including the preparation of this study, the Interstate Conflict Datasets Catalog (ICDC). The second major DDIR function was to begin addressing a set of longer-term support needs in emerging areas such as daily events data, and data in the general area of international political economy (IPE).

Fourteen dataset projects are currently supported under the umbrella DDIR Project (i.e., the data projects referred to earlier as being in the first domain of the DDIR Project). These datasets focus primarily on two types of information: (a) intra- and inter-state conflict, and (b) the national attributes of countries, as given by sociopolitical indicators. This book covers only a subset of the former class of these datasets—the interstate conflict datasets—for the purpose of documenting this key group of datasets in a scientifically useful, systematic fashion.

1.2.2   The Interstate Conflict Datasets

Eight DDIR interstate conflict datasets fall within the scope of this book. For practical operational purposes having to do with the organization of data collection, these eight DDIR interstate conflict datasets are actually grouped under six ongoing research projects, as listed in Table 1.1. The six projects focus on two classes of international conflict phenomena that are distinguishable by their magnitude or severity in terms of social violence taking place in the interaction. Although the exact type of conflict event contained in each of the eight datasets has its own operational definition (as shown in the next two chapters), the two main classes of events can be characterized as *potentially severe* international conflicts and *severe* international conflicts.

Table 1.1   DDIR Interstate Conflict Dataset Projects

DDIR Project Number and Name[a]	Principal Investigator(s)
POTENTIALLY SEVERE INTERNATIONAL CONFLICT: CRISES AND INTERVENTIONS	
10. Militarized Disputes Dataset of the COW Project	J. David Singer Charles Gochman and Zeev Maoz
5. International Crisis Behavior Project[b]	Jonathan Wilkenfeld
8. Interventions Project	Frederic S. Pearson
SEVERE INTERNATIONAL CONFLICT: WARS	
4. Great-Power War Project[b]	Jack S. Levy
9. Major-Minor Power War Project	Manus I. Midlarsky
7. Interstate War Dataset of the COW Project	J. David Singer
DATASET DOCUMENTATION	
6. Interstate War Catalog Project	Claudio Cioffi-Revilla

Source: From information published in *DDIR-Update* 1(1) October 1986, p. 3.

[a]Minor inconsistencies sometimes exist between the project names appearing in the cited issue of *DDIR-Update* and the name of projects as given by the principal investigators themselves.   Generally, the terminology found in this book uses the name used by the principal investigators.

[b]Projects 4 and 5 actually contain two datasets, each of which may be used independently of the other.

Potentially severe international conflicts are adversary international interactions (often involving tacit or explicit bargaining) that owe their scientific and policy relevance—among other features—to the fact that such interactions, when they initiate, have a greater-than-zero probability of escalating to a state of hostility designated as war (and a complementary probability of de-escalating). Such episodes are often called crises, and they may or may not take the form of military interventions or other uses of military force.

Severe international conflicts, on the other hand, are those violent social interactions that owe their significance to the fact that they always give rise to violent deaths of some magnitude, as a result of the organized exercise of military force with the intent to kill and destroy assets of an adversary. These severe episodes of international conflict are commonly called wars.

The research importance and scientific significance of the eight datasets generated by the six DDIR projects shown in Table 1.1 is largely self-evident to most empirically oriented international relations scholars. To others less familiar with this interdisciplinary area of social science research their relevance may be less obvious. Aside from allowing many different types of investigations of international conflict and peace patterns using a set of well-established statistical approaches (e.g., regression techniques of bi- and multivariate analysis), these data also have rapidly growing significance for their use in connection to mathematical modeling aimed at developing theory. In particular, these datasets are of great value for the application of formal approaches based on mathematical probability models (e.g., political reliability theory, event history analysis, survival modeling, success/failure analysis, and others), because they yield the most reliable estimates available on a large class of events connected with international conflict and peace. This book seeks to provide a useful description (Chapter 2) and a preliminary comparative analysis (Chapter 3) of those scientific aspects of each dataset deemed to be most crucial from a number of perspectives. The book itself may thus be viewed as being about "a dataset of datasets," with $N = 8$ datasets (or cases), and a preliminary comparative analysis of these datasets.

All in all the availability of this family of datasets opens up some new and exciting research frontiers in the scientific analysis of international security—as scientific observational projects often do. Because of this, the datasets described in this book are also of significant applied interest to international officials and analysts—particularly those concerned with monitoring and assessing requirements in the area of global international security policy. These data offer innovative means and methods for scientifically informing policy on a more rational basis than is customary in the world today. To dismiss this type of information as being mainly of "academic" or "historical" interest, as some public officials and institutions have in the past, is analogous to saying that long-range climatological data are worthless for improving global environmental policy. Although primarily created for purely scientific purposes, these datasets also have an undeniable public policy value of considerable magnitude, and one that remains greatly underutilized. With informed and skillful use, these datasets may provide an important contribution to increasing international stability through monitoring and early warning of potentially severe international situations.

The next chapter explains in detail the rationale behind and the descriptive profile of each of the eight datasets subsumed under the six DDIR projects listed in Table 1.1. The third chapter contains a set of comparative assessments across all eight datasets, with a view toward making them more scientifically useful to those who may wish to consider them in research.

2

The Interstate Conflict Datasets Catalog: Information Profiles

This chapter contains a set of detailed information profiles that describe the eight DDIR international conflict datasets identified in Chapter 1. The first section motivates and explains the new Interstate Conflict Datasets Catalog (ICDC) standard—the information format used in this chapter to describe datasets for purposes of research and preliminary comparisons. The new ICDC standard was designed as part of DDIR Project 6, the Interstate War Catalog, and is used later in this chapter for describing each dataset. The second and third sections of this chapter contain the actual information profiles, based on the ICDC standard. The eight information profiles are grouped by conflict types (potentially severe and severe types of international conflict), one type in each section, in the same manner as these were grouped earlier in Table 1.1.

All bibliographic references cited in the information profile pertaining to each dataset (i.e., those cited in Sections 2.2 and 2.3) are listed in the combined References section at the end of the book. As before, all other references are cited in footnotes.

2.1   Introduction

2.1.1   Describing Research Datasets in International Relations

Unlike conventional printed documents such as books and articles, a dataset residing in the memory of a computer is an information entity that poses some new and special problems as far as its scientific description and documentation is concerned. In a sense, the only way to describe it—to someone who is not familiar with what it contains, or with how it is

11

organized—is to "model" it, using some representational structure containing a set of information elements called fields of information.

Generally speaking, standard printed references used in connection with scientific research employ simple fields of information such as author(s) name(s), date and place of publication, title, number of pages, and so on. For datasets of measurements used in scientific investigation, however, the choice of a proper set of descriptive dimensions is far more dependent on practical considerations and available information. For example, whereas for a book (even in the case of a famous work) most scientists will not be interested in the names and references of others who have used such a book (assuming such information were available), in the case of a dataset such information on previous uses and applications can be very useful, indeed vital, in learning about ways in which the dataset in question has been used, or it may be critical for obtaining direct practical advice on the analytic potential and limitations of the dataset.

Simple descriptive problems such as the ones just mentioned (chosing a proper descriptive structure of information) may often be compounded in new interdisciplinary areas of research such as this—at the nexus between international relations, world politics, conflict and peace research—where there is no professionally set scientific standard for describing electronic media such as datasets, computer programs and graphic files.

2.1.2   The General ANSI Standard

In 1977 a general information standard of reference for describing data files in all fields of science was proposed by the American National Standards Institute (ANSI).[1] As with other ANSI standards, the purpose was to improve the documentation, storage, and retrieval of information about existing data files in any area of research.

Although the ANSI standard presents some advantages (primarily, it provides an initial benchmark where one did not previously exist) its use for this project presented several major drawbacks, which led to an early decision not to use it. First and foremost, in its present version the ANSI standard for data files does not seem very informative from the perspective of potential users of these social science datasets. For example, using the ANSI standard, one of the richest datasets of this project, the COW 10; SS1/5: Interstate Wars dataset, would be described roughly as follows:

---

[1]American National Standards Institute (1977), *American National Standard for Bibliographic References* (New York: American National Standards Institute).

> Correlates of War File I: Interstate Wars [Dataset]. From:
> Singer, J. David and Melvin Small, principal investigators.
> Resort to Arms.   Beverly Hills, CA: Sage; 1983. 1 1/4" tape;
> n tracks; ascii. [notes, etc.]

Clearly, such an information profile is too austere for the type of scientific research datasets covered by DDIR Project 6. The ANSI standard might suffice for describing some other, simpler databanks, such as the Index file of the *New York Times*.

Second, even when expanded to contain a few other information fields—such as "notes," "abstract," and a few other possibilities that are allowed—the ANSI standard is relatively unknown in the social sciences, although it appears to be used in several branches of engineering and physical sciences.

Finally, the fields of information in the ANSI standard, as well as their structure, seem to favor those datasets that have already appeared in printed form (as in the above example for COW 10; SS1/5). As a result of these and other considerations, there seemed little incentive to adopt the ANSI standard for this project at this stage. Perhaps the standard will be improved to make it more practical and informative in the not too distant future.

2.1.3   The Specialized ICDC Standard

The dataset profiles described in this chapter are based on the new ICDC standard, a more specialized information standard than the general ANSI standard for data files. As with other information standards, the ICDC standard is composed of a common set of basic dimensions to compare information across data sets.

The ICDC standard is a more specialized standard than the ANSI's because its principal purpose is to help increase and disseminate the quantity and quality of information specific to each of the eight interstate conflict datasets of the DDIR Project. This new specialized standard was necessary because the character of these datasets is new and relatively unknown in the research community.   Another purpose of the ICDC is to render such information comparable for further analysis whenever possible.   Although other information structures or media for representing the information are surely possible (e.g., using a hypertext file, such as a HyperCard™ stack or a SuperCard™ file running on an Apple Macintosh™), the ICDC standard aims at providing quick, easy, clear access to most of the essential information about the DDIR datasets.

The ICDC standard used for describing the eight interstate conflict datasets from a comparative perspective contains a total of 21 fields of descriptive information (both qualitative and quantitative). These 21 information fields may be described in terms of a codesheet model, as shown in Figure 2.1. They are defined as follows:

```
Dataset  Name
DDIR  ID      Event  Type    Info.  Update    IHCD ID
Principal  Investigator(s)
Generic  Event      Historic  Era  Begins        Ends
Event   Definition
Source  of  Event  Definition
Number  of  Events
Actor(s)
Target(s)
Event   Fields
Event   Source(s)
Published  Data  Source
Applied   Publications
Access  to  M.R.-Format
Remarks
References
```

Figure 2.1 *Codesheet model for describing a dataset according to the ICDC standard.*

Dataset Name: Name of the dataset. When an inconsistency exists between the DDIR name and the name most commonly used by the principal investigators, preference was given to the latter.

DDIR ID: This is the official number assigned to each DDIR Sub-Project, following the convention published in *DDIR-UPDATE*, vol. 1, no. 1, October 1986, p. 3.

Event Type: Fine (F) or coarse (C) types of conflict events, depending on the time-aggregation of the basic events (cases) coded in the dataset. All eight datasets in this catalog are coarse, although several of them contain fine events within the coarse events, which provide the basic unit of coding. Daily events datasets, such as those contained in the World Event Interactions Survey (WEIS) or in the Conflict and Peace Data Bank (COPDAB) are said to contain fine events.

Info. Update: The date of the most recent update of the information given in the dataset profile. Dates are given as six digits: YYMMDD, which stand for year, month, and day. The dates of these information profiles are all in the early- or mid-1989 range, when the final updates to the ICDC were made.

IHCD ID: The reference code of the dataset according to the *International Handbook of Conflict Datasets* (*IHCD*) (Cioffi-Revilla 1989c). The *IHCD* presently contains entries describing over 60 datasets gathered by conflict and peace researchers worldwide, and is currently being prepared for publication as part of the scientific documentation activity of the Long-Range Analysis of War (LORANOW) project at the University of Colorado at Boulder.

Principal Investigator(s): Name(s), address(es), and telephone number(s) of the principal investigator(s), along with computer mail addresses (E-mail), whenever possible. The exact form of a E-mail address may vary, depending on the sender's local system and/or the routing networks being used (e.g., Bitnet, Internet, EARN, etc.).

Generic Event: A brief descriptive label for the type of conflict event contained in the dataset. For this group of datasets this field may assume one of three possible values: war, crisis, or military intervention. Although these labels may appear arbitrary in some cases, they generally reflect some substantive (and/or conceptual) difference in the conflict origin, magnitude, or political consequences of the events in question.

Historic Era Begins: Calendar date (year) of the start of the collection (i.e., first date of the actual temporal coverage for the project). Note that the date of the very first event contained in the dataset may come some time after a dataset's start of historical coverage.

Ends: Date of the end of the collection (i.e., last date of the temporal range). The year cited in this field is inclusive.

Event Definition: Operational definition of the basic event unit (type of international conflict) contained in the dataset. This definition was taken, whenever possible, from the dataset's codebook; otherwise, it was obtained from direct communications with the principal investigator of the project. However, in some instances editing was carried out in the interest of greater definitional clarity, or the definition was actually constructed from the available documentation. (Event definitions used in the eight DDIR datasets are analyzed and compared later in Chapter 3, in the section on Concept Formation and comparative analysis [Section 3.5].)

Source of Event Definition: Project source(s) used for the event definition given in the immediately previous item (**Event Definition**).

Number of Events: Number of events contained in the dataset.

Actor(s):   Social units identified as agents of the conflict events contained in the dataset. This generally refers to the universe (class) of actors considered by the dataset as agents of conflict.

Target(s):   In these datasets the set of targets is usually—not always—the same as the set of actors. (In some events datasets, such as COPDAB, these two sets—the set of actors and the set of targets—are not identical.)

Event Fields: List of the variables coded or measured for each event contained in the dataset. The Stevens level-of-measurement of the values that these variables assume is generally nominal or ratio (cardinal). The name of each *variable* is given in italics. By convention, *units* of measurement, or special values assumed by a variable, are given within brackets [in Roman characters]. The following abbreviation [ymd] means that the value of a time variable (e.g., event duration) is given with a precision of year, month, and day. The operational definition of each variable in the dataset is not explicitly given in the profile, but may be found in the bibliographic references (or may be obtained directly from the principal investigators).

Event Source(s):   Historical and other source(s) used by the dataset project to obtain the events contained in the dataset.

Published Data Source: Printed publication(s), if any, where the raw dataset may be found.

Applied Publications: A selection of research publications that have used the dataset. Although a real effort was made to provide as complete a listing as possible—so that users may gain greater familiarity with the dataset, and perhaps discover other possible uses—no claim can be made of exhaustiveness.

Access to M.R.-Format: The status of the dataset in terms of machine-readable form. The ICPSR (Inter-University Consortium for Political and Social Research) file number is given whenever possible. For machine-readable files, additional information may be obtained in ICPSR, *Guide to Resources and Services* (yearly), (P.O. Box 1248, Ann Arbor, MI 48106). The Internet/BITNET address for ICPSR is ICPSR_NETMAIL@UM.CC.UMICH.EDU

Remarks: Any remarks about the dataset.

References: All references cited in the profile of a dataset are listed in full in the combined bibliography given in the Reference section at the end of the book. References to articles in periodicals appear in the citation standard of the *International Political Science Abstracts* adopted by the International Political Science Association.

The next two sections of this chapter use the ICDC standard to describe each of the eight international conflict datasets.

2.2 Potentially Severe
Interstate Conflict Events:
Crises and Military Interventions

As illustrated earlier in Table 1.1, the first set of four DDIR interstate conflict datasets concerns potentially severe conflicts with an intensity lower than war. This class of interstate conflict events is generally designated as crises (short of war) or as military interventions. Although these events have a conflict intensity lower than war, they are nonetheless potentially severe, since they may escalate to war—as many indeed do.

The four datasets in this class are the following:

1. COW 10: Militarized Interstate Disputes dataset of the Correlates of War Project (SS4/8)

2. Wilkenfeld 5A: International Crises dataset of the International Crisis Behavior (ICB) Project (JW1/28)

3. Wilkenfeld 5B: Foreign Policy Crises dataset of the International Crisis Behavior (ICB) Project (JW2/28)

4. Pearson 8: International Military Interventions dataset (FP1/32).

The information profile of each of these four datasets, using the ICDC standard, is given next.

The Correlates of War (COW) Project:
Militarized Interstate Disputes Dataset

DDIR ID	Event type	Info. update	IHCD ID
COW 10	C	891024	SS4/8

Principal investigator(s)
J. DAVID SINGER (Dept. of Political Science, 5602 Haven Hall, University of Michigan, Ann Arbor, MI 48109-1045. Tel. 313–763–6590), MELVIN SMALL (Dept. of History, Wayne State University, Detroit, MI 48202), CHARLES S. GOCHMAN (Dept. of Political Science, University of Pittsburgh, Pittsburgh, PA 15260. Tel. 412–648–7271), and ZEEV MAOZ (Dept. of Political Science, University of Haifa, Haifa, 31–999, Israel)

Internet/Bitnet: J_David_Singer@ub.cc.umich.edu and
          Gochman%pittsvms.bitnet@cornellc.ccs.cornell.edu

Generic event	Historic era begins	Ends
Crisis	1816	1988

Event definition
International disputes are distinguished from international wars in that fewer than 1,000 total fatalities are incurred by all the disputants involved, and at least one of the following events of military confrontation occurred: (1) explicitly threatened to resort to military force; or (2) mobilized, deployed, or otherwise displayed military force; or (3) actually resorted to military force short of war.

Sources of event definition
Singer (1979: 10), Singer and Small (1984)

Number of events
961 (up to 1976)

Actor(s)
Nation-state members of the international system

Target(s)
Nation-states

Event fields
[51 variable fields/record] *event* [dispute] *number, participant nations, level of hostility reached by each participant, major power involvement, onset date*

[ymd], *termination date* [ymd], *number of non-civilian fatalities, special characteristics of the dispute, outcome of the dispute* [war/peace]

Event source(s)
Numerous sources listed in Maoz (1982: 262–264). Complete list of sources available from the P.I.s.

Published data source
Singer and Small (1984)

Applied publications
Allan (1979), Bremer (1982), Bremer and Cusack (1980), Cioffi-Revilla (1985a, 1987), Cioffi-Revilla and Dacey (1988), Cusack and Eberwein (1980, 1982), Eberwein (1981), Gochman and Maoz (1984, 1989), Jones (1987), Leng and Gochman (1982), Maoz (1982, 1983a,b), Midlarsky (1989c), Stoll (1977, 1983, 1984a,b), Wayman et al. (1983), Williamson et al. (1988)

Access to M.R.-format
ICPSR file no. 9044 (*Wages of War, 1816–1980: Augmented with Disputes and Civil War Data. Part 3: Interstate Disputes*). Available from the ICPSR in both card image and OSIRIS formats.

Remarks
Russell J. Leng (Dept. of Political Science, Middlebury College) has also developed a related dataset (the Behavioral Correlates of War [B-COW] Project) containing fine-grained events data within each dispute episode. The B-COW dataset, along with other international conflict and cooperation datasets, will be described in equal detail in Cioffi-Revilla (1989c).

The *outcome* variable codes whether or not each dispute (crisis) in the COW 10 dataset escalated to war; this dataset may be used in combination with COW 7, which contains all the wars originating from the disputes in this dataset.

The following improvements to this dataset are planned under DDIR Sub-Project 10: "Collaboration with Charles Gochman to compare existing datasets on interstate disputes, revalidate and update militarized interstate dispute dataset, 1816–1988, and code additional variables (e.g., nature and stability of participating regimes, classification of disputes by issue area, third-party mediation)" (see *DDIR-UPDATE* 1(1) October 1986: 3).

References
See References section at the end of this book.

The International Crisis Behavior (ICB) Project: *International Crises* Dataset

DDIR ID	Event type	Info. update	IHCD ID
Wilkenfeld 5A	C	890514	JW1/28

Principal investigator(s)
MICHAEL BRECHER (Dept. of Political Science, McGill University, Montreal, Quebec, Canada H3A 2T7) and JONATHAN WILKENFELD (Dept. of Government and Politics, University of Maryland, College Park, MD 20742. Tel. 301–454–6729)

Internet/Bitnet: Wilkenfeld@umd2.umd.edu

Generic event	Historic era begins	Ends
Crisis	1929	1985

Event definition
An international crisis is a situational change characterized by two necessary and sufficient conditions: (1) distortion in the type and an increase in the intensity of disruptive interactions between two or more adversaries, with an accompanying high probability of military hostilities, or, during a war, an adverse change in the military balance; and (2) a challenge to the existing structure of an international system—global, dominant or subsystem—posed by the higher-than-normal conflictual interactions.

Source of event definition
Brecher, Wilkenfeld, and Moser (1988: 3)

Number of events
323

Actor(s)
Nation-states

Target(s)
Nation-states

Event fields
Data have been collected on two sets of variables: crisis attributes and crisis dimensions.

For the international crisis as a whole, there are seven clusters of crisis dimensions: (1) setting, (2) breakpoint-exitpoint, (3) crisis management technique, (4) great power/superpower activity, (5) international and regional organization involvement, (6) outcome, and (7) severity. Each cluster contains one or more specific variables. There are also six controls (crisis attributes): (1) geography, (2) polarity, (3) system level, (4) conflict, (5) power discrepancy, and (6) involvement by powers.

Event source(s)

Memoirs, books, official documents, scholarly articles, newspapers, the *New York Times Index,* and *Keesing's Contemporary Archives.* Works by area-specialist scholars were also used as sources of events (Brecher, Wilkenfeld, and Moser 1988: 29–30).

Published data source

Brecher, Wilkenfeld, and Moser (1988)

Applied publications

Brecher and Wilkenfeld (1982, 1989), Brecher and James (1986), Brecher, Wilkenfeld, and Moser (1988), Wilkenfeld and Brecher (1982, 1984), Wilkenfeld, Brecher, and Moser (1988)

Access to M.R.-format

A dataset file named CRISBANK, at the ICB Project of the University of Maryland, was referenced in Brecher and Wilkenfeld (1982: 393, 398). This ICB dataset is available from the ICPSR.

Remarks

Although this is essentially a dataset of coarse crisis events, each event contains temporal detail, i.e. triggering act, major response(s), termination mode, and so forth. Revalidation of this dataset, 1929–1979, and updating through 1985, is currently under way within DDIR Sub-Project 5 (principal investigator: J. Wilkenfeld). Note that the ICB Project encompasses two major datasets: dataset DDIR 5A (JW1/28), containing "international crises;" and DDIR 5B (JW2/28), containing "foreign policy crises."

References

See References section at the end of this book.

The International Crisis Behavior (ICB) Project: *Foreign Policy Crises* Dataset

DDIR ID	Event type	Info. update	IHCD ID
Wilkenfeld 5B	C	891024	JW2/28

Principal investigator(s)
MICHAEL BRECHER (Dept. of Political Science, McGill University, Montreal, Quebec, Canada H3A 2T7) and JONATHAN WILKENFELD (Dept. of Government and Politics, University of Maryland, College Park, MD 20742. Tel. 301–454–6729)

Internet/Bitnet: Wilkenfeld@umd2.umd.edu

Generic event	Historic era begins	Ends
Crisis	1929	1985

Event definition
A foreign policy crisis (i.e., a crisis viewed from the perspective of an individual state) is a situation with three necessary and sufficient conditions related to a change in a state's external or internal environment. All three are perceptions held by the highest level decisionmakers of the actor concerned: (1) a threat to basic values, (2) an awareness of finite time for response to the external value threat, and (3) a high probability of involvement in military hostilities.

Source of event definition
Wilkenfeld, Brecher, and Moser (1988: 3)

Number of events
698

Actor(s)
Nation-states

Target(s)
Nation-states

Event fields
Data have been collected on four sets of variables: *actor attributes* and *actor dimensions* (two sets of variables at the micro/state level); and *crisis*

attributes and *crisis dimensions* (two sets of variables at the macro/international level).

There are five clusters of *actor dimensions*: (1) *trigger*, (2) *actor behavior*, (3) *great power/superpower activity*, (4) *international and regional organization involvement*, and (5) *outcome*; each cluster contains one or more variables. Control variables include: macro-level controls (geography, polarity, system level, conflict, power discrepancy, and involvement by powers) and actor attribute controls (age, territory, regime, capability, values, and conditions). Also recorded is the peace/war outcome of the event.

Event source(s)
Memoirs, books, official documents, scholarly articles, newspapers, the *New York Times Index,* and *Keesing's Contemporary Archives.* Works by area-specialist scholars were also used as sources of events (Brecher, Wilkenfeld, and Moser 1988: 29–30).

Published data source
Wilkenfeld, Brecher, and Moser (1988)

Applied publications
Brecher and Wilkenfeld (1982, 1989), Brecher and James (1986), Brecher, Wilkenfeld, and Moser (1988), Creary and Wilkenfeld (1983), Wilkenfeld and Brecher (1982, 1984), Wilkenfeld, Brecher, and Moser (1988)

Access to M.R.-format
A dataset file named CRISBANK, at the ICB Project of the University of Maryland, is referenced in Brecher and Wilkenfeld (1982: 393, 398). This ICB dataset is available from the ICPSR.

Remarks
Although this is essentially a dataset of coarse crisis events, each event contains temporal detail, such as triggering act, major response(s), termination mode, and so forth. Revalidation of this dataset, 1929–1979, and updating through 1985, is currently under way within DDIR Sub-Project 5 (principal investigator: J. Wilkenfeld). Note that the ICB Project encompasses two major datasets: dataset DDIR 5A (JW1/28), containing "international crises;" and DDIR 5B (JW2/28), containing "foreign policy crises."

References
See References section at the end of this book.

International Military Interventions Dataset

DDIR ID	Event type	Info. update	IHCD ID
Pearson 8	C	890423	FP1/32

Principal investigator(s)
FREDERIC S. PEARSON (Dept. of Political Science, 8001 Natural Bridge Road, University of Missouri-St. Louis, St. Louis, MO 63121. Tel. 314–553–5755)

Internet/Bitnet: C18Ø4@umslvma

Generic event	Historic era begins	Ends
Military interventions	1946	1988

Event definition
International military interventions involve the movement of troops or forces of one independent country into the territory or territorial waters of another independent country, or military action by troops already stationed by one country inside another, in the context of some political issue or dispute.

Source of event definition
Pearson (1987: 1)

Number of events
> 200

Actor(s)
Nation-states

Target(s)
Nation-states

Event fields
Target country, intervener country, date intervention begins [ymd], *date intervention ends* [ymd], *source of intervention, type of military action* [troop intervention, aircraft incursion, naval force deployment, shelling], *primary datum source, colonial history?, power size of target, power size of intervener, type of intervention, contiguity, alignment of target*

Event source(s)
General sources: *The Economist, Facts on File, Foreign Affairs* (yearly chronology), *Newsweek*, the *New York Times*, the *New York Times Index*, the *St. Louis Post-Dispatch*, and the *Wall Street Journal*. Specific sources: Blechman and Kaplan (1978), Butterworth (1976), Center for Defense Information (1983), Donelan and Grieve (1973), Duner (1985), Eckhardt and Azar (1978), Kende (1971, 1978), Luard (1970), Maoz (1982), Northedge and Donelan (1971), Schmid and Berends (1985), Singer and Small (1972), Small and Singer (1982), Tillema (1973, 1986), Tillema and Van Wingen (1982), Van Wingen and Tillema (1980), and Zacher (1979). Numerous other regional sources are cited in Pearson (1987: 6–9).

Published data source
Dataset for 1948–1967 was reported in Pearson (1973).

Applied publications
Pearson (1974, 1984)

Access to M.R.-format
Not yet established

Remarks
The following improvements of this dataset are planned under DDIR Sub-Project 8: "Filling in dataset on unilateral, multilateral, and international organizational interventions, 1948–67, and updating through 1988; variables include effects of interventions, durations, and measures of magnitude" (see *DDIR-UPDATE* 1(1) October 1986: 3).

References
See References section at the end of this book.

2.3   Severe Interstate Conflict Events: Wars

The second set of four DDIR interstate conflict datasets concerns conflicts that exhibit the character and intensity of war. This class of interstate conflict events is distinguished by its particularly severe intensity and magnitude. Unlike crises or interventions, events in this class *always* result in significant loss of human life in the range of approximately 1,000 fatalities or higher, depending on the operational definition of war. Also, as noted earlier in Section 2.2, almost all events in this class originate from international crises or from interventions that are not resolved by peaceful means; they sometimes result from both.

Following the grouping in Table 1.1, the four datasets in this second class are the following:

1. Levy 4A: Interstate Wars Involving the Great Powers dataset (JL1/18)

2. Levy 4B: Great Power Wars dataset (JL2/18)

3. Midlarsky 9: Major-minor Power War dataset (ML1/54)

4. COW 7: Interstate Wars dataset of the Correlates of War project (SS1/5)

The ICDC information profile for each of these datasets is given next.

Interstate Wars Involving the Great Powers Dataset

DDIR ID	Event type	Info. update	IHCD ID
Levy 4A	C	891018	JL1/18

Principal investigator(s)
JACK S. LEVY (Dept. of Political Science, Hickman Hall, Rutgers University, New Brunswick, NJ 08903. Tel. 201–932–9262)

Generic event	Historic era begins	Ends
War	1495	1975

Event definition
A substantial armed conflict between the organized military forces of independent political units; interstate wars [in the sense of Small and Singer (1982)] involving at least one "great power."

Source of event definition
Levy (1983a: 51); the definition of a "great power" is found in Levy (1983a: ch. 2).

Number of events
119

Actor(s)
Every actor or target (or both) always belongs to the set of "great powers" in the international system (viz., France, England/Great Britain [United Kingdom], Spain, Austrian Hapsburgs/Austria/Austria-Hungary [Austria, Hungary], Ottoman Empire [Turkey], United Hapsburgs, Netherlands, Sweden, Russia/Soviet Union, Prussia/Germany/Federal Republic of Germany, Italy, United States, Japan, China), although the period of membership in "the great power system" varies for each actor.

Target(s): Nation-states

Event fields
Event [war] *number, event* [war] *name, onset date* [ymd], *termination date* [ymd], *duration* [days], *extent* [number of belligerent great powers], *magnitude* [nation-years], *severity* [combatant fatalities], *intensity* [(combatant fatalities)/(European population) = *severity*/(European

population)], *concentration* [(combatant fatalities)/(nation-years) = *severity/magnitude*]

Event source(s)
Bodart (1916), Dumas and Vedel-Peterson (1923), Dupuy and Dupuy (1977), Harbottle (1967), Langer (1972), Richardson (1960), Singer and Small (1972), Sorokin (1937), Woods and Baltzly (1915), and Wright (1942). See Levy (1983a: 55–57)

Published data source
Levy (1983a: 88–91)

Applied publications
Cioffi-Revilla (1985b, 1986, 1988a), Goldstein (1985, 1987, 1988), Levy (1981, 1982a,b, 1983a,b, 1984a,b, 1985a,b), Levy and Morgan (1984, 1986a), Modelski and Morgan (1985), Morgan and Levy (1986, 1989), Thompson (1985)

Access to M.R.-format
(1) An Apple Macintosh™ file prepared by T. Clifton Morgan is available from the principal investigator; (2) a StatView™ or a DataDesk™ file (filename = LEVY), in Apple Macintosh™ versions, are available from the author.

Remarks
Variables other than those described above (see **Event fields**), as well as missing data for existing variables, are being added to this dataset under DDIR Sub-Project 4.

References
See References section at the end of this book.

Great Power Wars Dataset

DDIR ID	Event type	Info. update	IHCD ID
Levy 4B	C	891018	JL2/18

Principal investigator(s)
JACK S. LEVY (Dept. of Political Science, Hickman Hall, Rutgers University, New Brunswick, NJ 08903. Tel. 201–932–9262)

Generic event	Historic era begins	Ends
War	1495	1975

Event definition
A substantial armed conflict between the organized military forces of independent national political units; interstate wars [in the sense of Small and Singer (1982)] involving at least one "great power" on each side.

Source of event definition
Levy (1983a: 51); see Levy (1983a: ch. 2) for the definition of "great power."

Number of events
60

Actor(s)
Every actor or target (or both) always belongs to the set of "great powers" in the international system [viz., France, England/Great Britain (United Kingdom), Spain, Austrian Hapsburgs/Austria/Austria-Hungary (Austria, Hungary), Ottoman Empire (Turkey), United Hapsburgs, Netherlands, Sweden, Russia/Soviet Union, Prussia/Germany/Federal Republic of Germany, Italy, United States, Japan, China], although the period of membership in "the great power system" varies for each actor.

Target(s)
Nation-states

Event fields
Event [war] *number, event* [war] *name, onset date* [ymd], *termination date* [ymd], *duration* [days], *extent* [number of belligerent great powers], *magnitude* [nation-years], *severity* [combatant fatalities], *intensity* [(combatant fatalities)/(European population) = *severity*/(European population)], *concentration* [(combatant fatalities)/(nation-years) = *severity/magnitude*]

Event source(s)
Over 400 sources were used; a complete listing (Levy 1989) is available from the principal investigator. A. D. Anderson (1956), M. S. Anderson (1954, 1966, 1978), R. C. Anderson (1952), I. Anderson (1956), Bain (1899), Barker (1975), Barton (1972), Bobrick (1987), Bodart (1916), Coughlan (1974), Creasy (1856), Dmytryshyn (1977), Duffy (1981), Dumas and Vedel-Peterson (1923), Dupuy and Dupuy (1977), Eversley and Chirol (1969), A. W. Fisher (1970), S. N. Fisher (1959), Grey (1973), Harbottle (1967), Hatton (1980), Israel (1982), Jones (1987), Kohn (1986), Langer (1972, 1980), Longworth (1984), Lord (1915), Maland (1980), McKay (1981), McKay and Scott (1983), McNeil (1964), Merriman (1944, 1962), Murray (1969), Naroll et al. (1974), Pitcher (1985), Polisensky (1970), Richardson (1960), Roberts (1968), Roider (1972), Schama (1987), Singer and Small (1972), Sorel (1898), Sorokin (1937), Spielman (1977), Tapie (1971), Waliszeski (1898), Wittek (1963), Woods and Baltzly (1915), and Wright (1942). See Levy (1983a: 55–57).

Published data source
Levy (1983a: 88–91)

Applied publications
Cioffi-Revilla (1985b, 1988a), Cioffi-Revilla et al. (1988), Goldstein (1985, 1987, 1988), Levy (1981, 1982a,b, 1983a,b, 1984a,b, 1985a,b), Levy and Morgan (1984, 1986), Modelski and Morgan (1985), and Morgan and Levy (1986, 1989)

Access to M.R.-format
An Apple Macintosh™ file prepared by T. Clifton Morgan is available from the principal investigator.

Remarks
Variables other than those described above (see **Event fields**), as well as missing data for existing variables, are being added to this dataset under DDIR Sub-Project 4. This dataset contains only great power wars, and is a subset of dataset JL1/18, *Interstate Wars Involving the Great Powers* (Levy 1983a), consisting of all great power wars in JL1/18 plus those of the period 1975–1985.

References
See References section at the end of this book.

Major-minor Power Wars Dataset

DDIR ID	Event type	Info. update	IHCD ID
Midlarsky 9	C	891018	ML1/54

Principal investigator(s)
MANUS I. MIDLARSKY (Dept. of Political Science, Hickman Hall, Rutgers University, New Brunswick, NJ 08903. Tel. 201–932–9262)

Generic event	Historic era begins	Ends
War	1495	1815

Event definition
Interstate wars [in the sense of Small and Singer (1982)] involving at least one "major" and one "minor" power.

Source of event definition
Midlarsky (1988a,b)

Number of events
154

Actor(s)
Major or minor powers (nation-states)

Target(s)
Major or minor powers (nation-states)

Event fields
Event [war] *number*, *event* [war] *name*, *date of onset* [year; month and day only for some wars], *participant belligerents* [major power(s), minor power (s)], *war initiator(s)*, *war location* [geographic region], *belligerents' population*, *belligerents' armed forces*, *war outcome*, *termination date* [year; month and day only for some wars], *battle fatalities* (only for some wars)

Event source(s)
Bair (1986), Banks (1971), Canby (1984), Dupuy and Dupuy (1977, 1986), Eggenberger (1967), *Encyclopedia Britannica* (1910), Harbottle (1971), Kohn (1986), Mitchell (1978), Russell (1958), Small and Singer (1982), *Stateman's Yearbook,* Symcox (1983), and Williams (1968, 1969)

Published data source
None as yet. A printout is available from the author.

Applied publications
None as yet

Access to M.R.-format
Available in 5.25 or 3.50" diskettes in ASCII format, in the same format as SS1/5. Codebook is Midlarsky and Park (1988).

Remarks
Development of this dataset is funded by DDIR Sub-Project 9 and is summarized as follows: "Identification and dating of wars between major and minor powers, 1495–1815, with respect to date of initiation, participation, termination for each participant, and, where possible, casualties" (*DDIR-UPDATE* 1(1) October 1986: 3).

References
See References section at the end of this book.

The Correlates of War (COW) Project:
Interstate Wars Dataset

DDIR ID	Event type	Info. update	IHCD ID
COW 7	C	891024	SS1/5

Principal investigator(s)

J. DAVID SINGER (Dept. of Political Science, 5602 Haven Hall, University of Michigan, Ann Arbor, MI 48109-1045. Tel. 313–763–6590), and MELVIN SMALL (Dept. of History, Wayne State University, Detroit, MI 48202)

Internet/Bitnet: J_David_Singer@ub.cc.umich.edu

Generic event	Historic era begins	Ends
War	1816	1986

Event definition

Sustained military combat involving regular armed forces of at least one sovereign state member of the international system against those of (a) another state member of the international system (interstate war), or (b) any forces of a nonstate entity (extra-systemic), resulting in at least 1,000 battle fatalities of belligerent combatants per year.

Source of event definition

Small and Singer (1982: 55), Singer (1989: 2)

Number of events

118 (67 intra-systemic wars, 51 extra-systemic wars)

Actor(s)

At least one (for extra-systemic) and one on each side (for interstate) must (during time of war) be nation-state members of the international system (Small and Singer, 1982: 47–50).

Target(s)

Actors and targets are specified in Small and Singer (1982: 47–50).

Event fields

Event [war] *number*, *event* [war] *name*, *war type* [interstate, colonial, imperial], *war location* [region(s) of fighting], *war participants*, *initiation date of war* [ymd], *initiation date of participants* [ymd], *termination date of war* [ymd], *termination date of participants* [ymd], *duration of war* [months], *pre-war population of participants* [inhabitants], *pre-war armed forces, war outcome for each participant* [win, lose, tie], *war initiator(s), magnitude* [nation-months], *severity* [battle fatalities of system member participants], *intensity* [(battle fatalities)/(nation-month); and (battle fatalities)/(10,000 population)]

Event source(s)
Numerous sources, cited in Small and Singer (1982: Appendix A, 297–313)

Published data source
Small and Singer (1982)

Applied publications
Altfeld and Bueno de Mesquita (1979), Attinà (1976), Bremer et al. (1973, 1975), Bueno de Mesquita (1978, 1980, 1981a,b, 1983, 1985), Bueno de Mesquita and Altfeld (1979), Bueno de Mesquita and Lalman (1986, 1988), Bueno de Mesquita and Singer (1973), Cannizzo (1978), Cioffi-Revilla (1985a, 1987), Cioffi-Revilla and Dacey (1988), Diehl (1983a,b, 1985a,b), Doran and Parsons (1980), Duncan and Siverson (1982), Eberwein (1981), Eberwein et al. (1976), Gleditsch and Singer (1975), Gochman (1975), Houweling and Kuné (1984), Job and Ostrom (1976), Leng and Goodsell (1974), Leng and Wheeler (1979), Midlarsky (1974, 1975, 1986a,b, 1989c), Mihalka (1976), Most and Starr (1980), Rapoport (1983: ch. 24), Ray (1974), Ray and Gochman (1979), Sabrosky (1976), Singer (1972, 1976, 1979a, 1980, 1981, 1982), Singer and Bouxsein (1975), Singer et al. (1972), Singer and Associates (1979), Singer and Cusack (1981), Singer and Small (1966, 1968, 1970, 1972, 1974), Singer and Stoll (1984), Singer and Wallace (1970, 1979), Siverson and King (1980), Siverson and Sullivan (1983), Siverson and Tennefoss (1982), Skjelsbaek (1972), Small (1976, 1978), Small and Singer (1970, 1976, 1979, 1982, 1989), Stoll (1982), Stoll and Champion (1977, 1985), Thompson (1982, 1985), Thompson et al. (1979), Vasquez (1976), Vayrynen (1983), Wallace (1971, 1972, 1973a,b, 1979, 1981, 1982), Wallensteen (1981), Wayman (1982, 1984), Wayman et al. (1983), Weede (1974, 1981, 1984), Westing (1982), Wheeler (1975), Wittman (1979)

Access to M.R.-format
ICPSR file no. 9044, part 1 (*The Wages of War, 1816–1980: Augmented with Disputes and Civil War Data*). Available from the ICPSR in both card image and OSIRIS formats. The 118 wars in this ICPSR dataset are not sorted by wars, but rather by system members.

Remarks

By far the most widely utilized social science dataset on severe international conflicts. SS1/5 includes both extra-systemic (imperial and colonial) as well as systemic wars. Extra-systemic wars are those in which the adversary is not a member of the international system but is an independent nonmember of the system or a nonindependent entity (Small and Singer 1982: 81). An interstate war is a war in which at least one participant on each side is a member of the international system. See also SS2 (Small and Singer 1982: 51). Extra-systemic wars are indicated as imperial or colonial (Small and Singer 1982: 79–80). Intra-systemic is the same as interstate (Singer 1989: 2).

Note that the *severity* of a war event in this dataset measures exclusively the battle fatalities incurred by the system-member participants only. Thus, such a measure does not count battle fatalities incurred by any nonmember of the international system that may have participated in the war. The *severity* measured in this dataset therefore underestimates the total battle fatalities of the war events comprised in the dataset. The empirical magnitude of such underestimation is presently unknown, and large disparities in the lethality of military weapons technology may give rise to very high fatalities on the part of nonsystem members.

Under DDIR Sub-Project 7, the following improvements of this dataset were undertaken: "updating, 1980–88, of COW dataset on initiation of interstate wars, participation (in nation-months), and casualties; defining and coding additional variables for 1816–1988 on monthly information on casualty rates, interventions by third parties, war phases, and characteristics of war terminations" (*DDIR-UPDATE* 1(1) Oct. 1986: 3).

References

See References section at the end of this book.

3
Comparative Analysis of Datasets

3.1 Introduction

This chapter presents some preliminary comparisons of the eight DDIR interstate conflict datasets described in the previous chapters. Aggregate comparisons are important not only for gaining a better understanding and an appreciation of the specific scientific contributions of each dataset, but also for purposes of assessing scientific progress and cumulation in this area of social science research and methodology. Another purpose of these cross-dataset comparisons is to provide some practical information for deciding which specific dataset(s) may be useful for some individual research project or analytic purpose.

Computer-based datasets are essentially multidimensional collections of information on electronic media, systematically organized by record-case, according to some set of consistent formatting principles to facilitate their practical use in analysis. Due to the considerable information diversity of these datasets, as well as the increasing diversity of potential users (academics, policy analysts, and others) with an interest in any given type or class of datasets, there are many possible ways in which these datasets may be compared. For instance, a practicing researcher will probably be primarily interested in learning more about how a class of datasets compares in actual information content or in coding reliability to other datasets. By contrast, a computer support specialist (perhaps a member of the same project group) will want to learn more information about memory space requirements, file formatting, and so forth.

The cross-dataset comparisons examined in this chapter focus on the following five basic dimensions of the DDIR interstate conflict dataset projects:

1. *Geographic* (or academic) *distribution and network topography* across the United States

2. *Space and time coverage* along the historical timeline

3. *Onset rates of conflict events* (or "behavioral density") recorded by each dataset

4. Logic of *concept formation* for the various types of conflict events ("comparative semantics")

5. Primary and secondary *documents and sources* used for collecting information contained in each dataset

Other comparative analyses are possible, so the ones presented in this chapter should be seen only as preliminary attempts with a view toward future refinements. Because it was not until recently that there existed a sufficient number of reliable datasets to draw some of these systematic comparisons, it is likely that soon other analysts will think of other comparisons and analyses. The future will probably witness other comparative assessments, particularly as these and other important datasets become more available and are used in various international research projects.

3.2 Geographic Distribution and Network Topography

The geographic distribution and university location of the eight interstate conflict dataset projects of the DDIR Project are represented in Figure 3.1. The figure shows a distribution of six projects in as many universities, extended over three different time zones in the continental United States—a fact to keep in mind for various communication and interaction purposes (e.g., electronic mail by Bitnet, Internet, or other networks). Researchers outside the continental United States should additonally consider the –5 hours time difference between the U.S. Eastern Standard Time (EST) zone and the Greenwich Mean Time (GMT) zone. Researchers in Asia should also keep in mind the change of date across the International Date Line (midnight GMT). Most Latin American countries are one or two hours east (ahead) of the U.S. EST zone, or +3 and +4 hours from U.S. Mountain Time zone.

The only dataset project that is currently distributed in more than one university research group is the Militarized Interstate Disputes dataset (DDIR 10; IHCD SS4/8) of the Correlates of War Project, projects at the University of Michigan at Ann Arbor (J. D. Singer) and at the University of Pittsburgh (C. S. Gochman). Also, due to the frequent movement of faculty and researchers in the U. S. academic community, the location of some projects

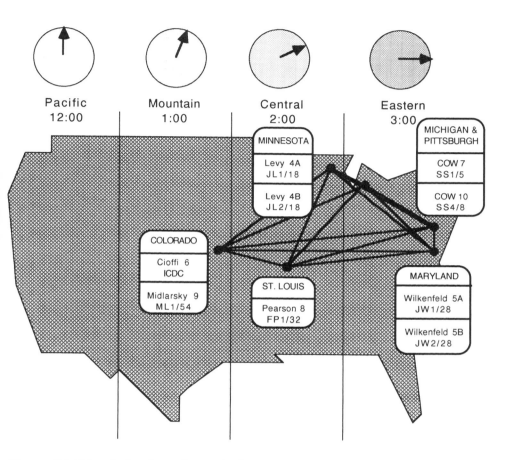

Figure **3.1** *University location and network of NSF-DDIR projects on Interstate Conflict datasets*

may change over time—even in the near future. In general, projects follow their principal investigator. For instance, while the DDIR dataset projects by J. S. Levy and M. I. Midlarsky were carried out at the University of Minnesota and the University of Colorado at Boulder, respectively, both researchers moved to Rutgers University while this book was being completed (see current addresses in Section 2.3). Both projects now reside at Rutgers.

The fast-growing Bitnet (Because-It-is-Time), Internet, and NSFNet telecommunications networks have provided—and will likely continue to provide—important channels of rapid and efficient scientific communication and exchange between these and other projects. Internet/Bitnet addresses for the project principal investigators were given earlier, when available (see the profile of each dataset in Sections 2.2 and 2.3). The Department of Political Science of the University of Kentucky also maintains an updated Bitnet directory of political scientists in the United States as well as in other countries. (For further information on the University of Kentucky E-mail directory, send a message to: POL101@UKCC.UKY.EDU).

3.3   Space and Time Coverage

Aside from subject matter, *space* and *time* coverage are perhaps the two most basic dimensions for comparing empirical datasets. For the eight interstate conflict datasets of the DDIR project, their "social space" is approximately the same—at least in broad qualitative terms—because all eight datasets are primarily designed to measure and record the conflict behavior of nation-states. On the other hand, their time coverage varies significantly.

3.3.1   Social Space: Types of Actors

The total social space, or universe of actors, of these datasets roughly corresponds to *the international system of nation-states at any given historical time, including both large and small nation-states.* The precise composition of the social space of each dataset actually varies across time periods (as the composition of the international system changes). All eight datasets are—exclusively and explicitly—datasets about interstate conflict behavior events. Later in this chapter, when we compare the various operational definitions of international conflict employed by each dataset (see Section 3.5 on Concept Formation), more will be said about the actual composition of the set of social actors (behavioral units) whose conflict behavior is recorded in these datasets.

As a consequence of the exclusive focus on nation-state actors, excluded from these datasets are all episodes of societal conflict (both severe and potentially severe) that are carried out by any other type of nonstate actor or agent, such as terrorist groups, violent social movements, guerrilla or revolutionary organizations (urban or rural). Thus, in comparative terms, the social space of these datasets is relatively homogeneous in a qualitative sense (i.e., involving only nation-state types of political systems as actors and targets of conflict behavior) but such a focus differs substantially with respect to other existing conflict datasets, which view conflict as a more universal societal phenomenon (e.g., L. F. Richardson's *Statistics of Deadly Quarrels* dataset, containing many intergroup conflict events involving nonstate actors).

Although all eight DDIR datasets record the foreign conflict behavior of national units (nation-state political systems), some important differences exist in the *types of national political units* included in each dataset. Ideally, a systematic treatment of the conflict behavior of these heterogeneous political units should be supported by some type of comprehensive taxonomy of political units—one based on sound theoretical principles. Such a taxonomy would facilitate meaningful comparisons, as did Aristotle's taxonomy of political systems until recent times. However, at present no such widely accepted taxonomy readily exists in contemporary political science (a lamentable deficiency of current theory!), so the most that can be said about the different types of political units in these datasets is that they range from "nation-state members of the international system" (which may be major or minor powers) to "great powers," according to the specification given in the operational definition of interstate conflict used in each dataset. It may therefore be concluded that *virtually all the war-like behavior, and some of the crisis-like behavior of nation-state members of the international system has now been recorded by these eight datasets*, for the periods of time (historical time ranges or "eras") discussed next.

As a corollary—in terms of the social space yet to be covered by future data collection projects on conflict and peace—it is clear that *crisis-type conflict events* and the highly significant class of *conflict events involving nonstate actors* (be they domestic or international) are the next areas of data collection for recent centuries. We shall return to this aspect in Section 3.5 (Concept Formation), when we discuss the operational definitions and conceptual logic structures associated with the various types of conflict events.

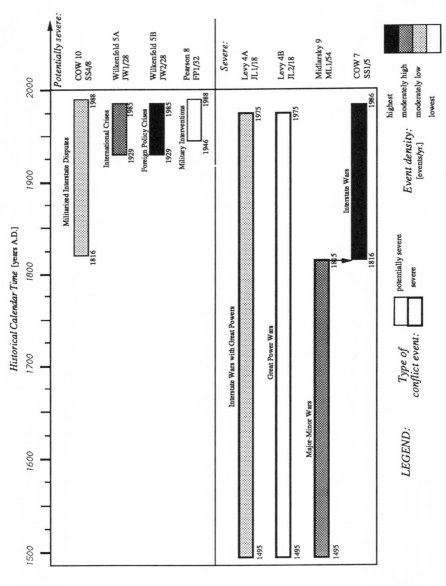

Figure 3.2 *Historical range of the DDIR interstate conflict datasets, 1495–1988 A.D.*

3.3.2   Historical Time Ranges

In contrast to the relative homogeneity of the social space covered by these datasets (consisting of national political units), some major cross-dataset differences exist in terms of historical time coverage. The temporal range of some projects may be measured in calendar time units of centuries (long-range scope); for others the temporal range is more appropriately measured in units of decades or years (medium- and short-range, respectively).

Figure 3.2 illustrates the historical calendar coverage of each dataset for a total timeline (top horizontal axis) that extends for almost half a millennium (1495 to 1988 A.D.). As can be seen from this time chart, longer coverage is characteristic of war-type datasets, whereas shorter coverage is more typical of crisis-type datasets. Thus, *the past five centuries of history are now well recorded in terms of the most severe, war-like phenomena among nations, and the last 170 years are well recorded (for national political units) for the lower range of conflict intensity* (crises and military interventions of subwar magnitude).

Figure 3.2 also shows the *relative density* of each dataset as measured in number of events per unit of time, grouped by the corresponding event magnitude (severe vs. potentially severe conflicts). As indicated in the figure, the *most dense* of these datasets are Wilkenfeld 5B (foreign policy crises) and COW 7 (interstate wars), for potentially severe and severe conflicts, respectively. The *least dense* are Pearson 8 (military interventions) and Levy 4B (great power wars), for crisis and war types, respectively.

With respect to other interstate conflict datasets—outside of the eight DDIR projects of the ICDC—only the War in Intergroup Relationships dataset (Sorokin 1937), and the Wars of Modern Civilization dataset of the Causes of War Project (Wright 1942) have similar or longer historical time ranges. The former dataset (500 B.C. to 1925 A.D.) covers a very limited set of nations and historical empires, whereas the latter (1480 A.D. to 1964 A.D.) is often viewed (somewhat erroneously) as based primarily on a definition of war too stringently dependent on the formal criteria of international law.[1]

---

[1] Another long-range study of war, deterrence, and territorial change is reported in Raoul Naroll et al.'s 1974 *Military Deterrence in History*, cited in the References. However, like Sorokin's dataset, the Naroll study includes only a limited set of actors, for a limited number of time intervals.

3.4   Onset Rates of Conflict Events

3.4.1   Onset Rate Estimates

Information about the historical range of an event dataset may be combined with information about the total number of events contained in the dataset to derive preliminary aggregate estimates for rates of onset for various types of interstate conflict. Such an onset rate (k) may also be interpreted as the "behavioral density" of a dataset because it is a measure of the number of conflict events per unit of time (conflict frequency).

Aggregate event rates for severe and potentially severe international conflicts in the eight DDIR datasets of the ICDC are reported in Table 3.1 and graphically depicted in Figure 3.3.

Table 3.1 shows a comparative summary of the number of international conflict events (N), the historic range ($\Delta t+1$), the estimated rate of onset (k), and the estimated mean time between events (MTBE) for each of the eight datasets. The cumulative for the number of events in the eight datsets shows that a total of more than 2,588 interstate conflict events in the global system were coded, for a total of 1,784 cumulative years of historical timeline. (The "half-life" of peace, defined by convention as $(\ln 2)/k$, may

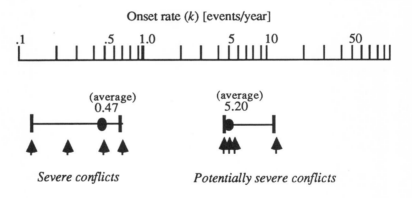

Figure 3.3 *Average and range of onset estimates* (k) *for severe (wars) and potentially severe (crises) international conflict events.*

also be calculated; however, the MTBE is sufficient for our present purposes.)[2]

To facilitate synthesis and comparison, the average and range of estimates reported in Table 3.1 are graphically illustrated in Figure 3.3, for both classes of international conflict—severe (war-type) and potentially severe (crisis-type) events.

It should be noted that these highly aggregated onset rates and MTBE estimates are calculated over the *entire historic range of each dataset*. In practice, as recent studies have shown (e.g., Cioffi-Revilla 1985; Houweling and Kuné 1984; Houweling and Faber 1984; Houweling and Siccama 1985), these parameter estimates are seldom stationary (typically, they are time-dependent) so different historical eras (time intervals) often yield different numerical values for these parameters. Interstate conflict, in summary, is a time-varying stochastic process (it may even have second-order, parametric stochasticity) *with average approximate event rates* as given in Table 3.1 and Figure 3.3.

By combining the dataset ranges and estimated onset rates reported in Table 3.1, we can obtain the distribution of datasets along the two dimensions (frequency and range). This is illustrated in Figure 3.4. As can be seen, two clusters of events are formed—potentially severe (*upper left*) and severe (*lower right*) international conflicts. Overall, crisis-type events have higher frequency (by an order of magnitude) and shorter historical coverage, whereas war-type events have lower frequency and longer time coverage. Viewing the eight datasets as a whole, event frequency is inversely related to historical coverage—as in some kind of "observational tradeoff," which tends to yield roughly the same average magnitude of events per event class. In a practical sense, this comparison between historical range of coverage, and event-type being coded, is useful to consider for purposes of planning future data collection projects—particularly when each dataset project is correlated with human and material resources consumed. Clearly, the coding of potentially severe conflicts (crises) in the fifteenth to the nineteenth centuries will require an unprecedented scientific effort.[3]

---

[2]The "half-life" of peace (or of war) is defined as the time interval required for the cumulative probability of war (or of peace) to reach a value of 0.5. Half-life estimates for peace and war in various eras of international history are reported in Cioffi-Revilla (1985a,b, 1986, 1988a, 1989a) and Cioffi-Revilla et al. (1988).

[3]If the 1816–1966 average onset rate of > 5.20 crises/year is any indication, then the last five centuries may contain > 260,000 crises, although the real number is likely to be smaller than this because of the smaller number of potentially interacting nations in the earlier historical period (16th–19th centuries).

Table 3.1   Aggregate rates of Interstate Conflict events, 1495–1988 A.D.

Dataset	Number of Events, N	Range of Years	Historic Range, $\Delta t + 1$ [years]	Onset Rate, $k = N(\Delta t + 1)$ [events per year]	Mean Time Between Events $1/k$ [years]
POTENTIALLY SEVERE CONFLICTS: CRISES AND INTERVENTIONS					
COW 10	> 916	1816–1988	173	> 5.29	< 0.189
Wilkenfeld 5A	323	1929–1985	57	5.67	0.176
Wilkenfeld 5B	698	1929–1985	57	12.25	0.082
Pearson 8	> 200	1946–1988	43	> 4.65	< 0.215
SUBTOTALS:	> 2,137	——	330	——	——
AVERAGES:[a]	480	——	82.5	> 5.20	< 0.192
SEVERE CONFLICTS: WARS					
Levy 4A	119	1495–1975	481	0.247	4.042
Levy 4B	60	1495–1975	481	0.125	8.017
Midlarsky 9	154	1495–1815	321	0.480	2.084
COW 7	118	1816–1986	171	0.690	1.449
SUBTOTALS:	451	——	1,454	——	——
AVERAGES:[b]	130	——	363.5	0.472	2.527
FOR ALL EVENTS:	> 2,588[c]	1495-1988	1,784	> 2.84[d]	< 1.36[e]

Source: Calculated by the author using information reported in Chapter 2.

[a]These estimates of potentially severe conflict are *systemic*, so they are calculated without using Wilkenfeld 5B, which contains nation-level events (Wilkenfeld 5A is systemic).

[b]Calculated without using the Levy 4B dataset, which is a subset of Levy 4A.

[c]Total number of international conflict events contained in the eight DDIR interstate conflict datasets.

[d]Average onset rate of international conflict events (counting both potentially severe and severe conflicts).

[e]Meantime between international conflict events (MTBE), counting both potentially severe and severe conflicts.

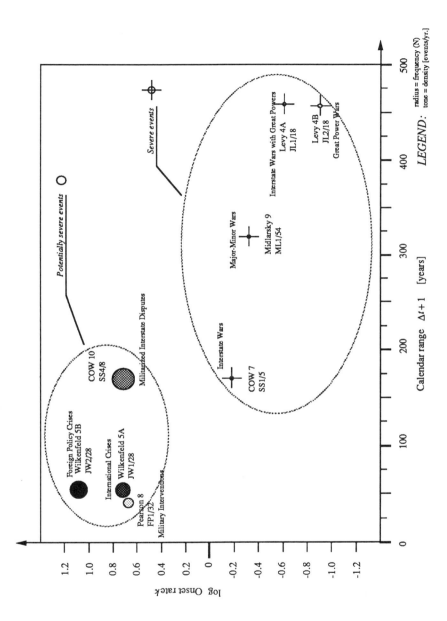

Figure 3.4 *Frequency-range diagram: Dataset clusters formed by different rate frequencies (log k) and calendar ranges.*

3.4.2 Empirical Equations for the Onset of International Conflict

Subject to the preceding caveats and reservations, the aggregate onset rate estimates derived from these datasets (values of the parameter k) are still meaningful and insightful. With due caution they may be used for some analytic purposes (Cioffi-Revilla, 1989a). For instance, as numerous previous studies (Cioffi-Revilla 1985a,b; Moyal 1949: 447; Richardson 1945a,b; Singer and Small, 1972) have shown, many types of interstate conflict processes have a distribution of times between onsets (when this is viewed as a random variable T), which can be approximately modeled by the Poisson process with cumulative density function (c.d.f.) $\Phi(t)$ given by

$$\Phi(t) = P(T \leq t)$$

$$= \int_{0}^{+\infty} p(t)\, \mathrm{d}t = 1 - e^{-kt}$$

and probability density function (p.d.f.) $p(t)$ given by

$$p(t) = \frac{\mathrm{d}}{\mathrm{d}t}\Phi(t) = k\,e^{-kt}.$$

(This model ignores the time-dependence, or nonstationarity mentioned earlier in Section 3.4.1.) The first of these equations (for the c.d.f.) describes the probability that a conflict will occur *by* some time t [years] since the previous onset. The second (for the p.d.f.) describes the probability (density) that the next onset will take place in the neighborhood of t [years].

Thus, using aggregate estimates of the parameter k [number of events per year], the corresponding empirical equations for the onset of crises and wars in the global system may be expressed as follows:

$$\textit{for crises:} \quad \left\{ \begin{array}{l} \Phi_{\text{crisis}}(t) \approx 1 - e^{-5.20t} \\[2mm] p_{\text{crisis}}(t) \approx 5.20\,e^{-5.20t} \end{array} \right\};$$

and

$$for\ wars: \left\{ \begin{array}{l} \Phi_{\text{war}}(t) \approx 1 - e^{-0.47t} \\ \\ p_{\text{war}}(t) \approx 0.47\ e^{-0.47t} \end{array} \right\}.$$

From a scientific viewpoint, these equations have considerable synthetic value because *they describe in the most general terms the empirical laws governing the onset of crises and wars from the most aggregate perspective* (ignoring nonstationarity). However, it must be reiterated that they are only generalizations that hold over relatively long periods of time. When particular historical eras are analyzed, values of the parameter k vary (and possibly the form of the equations as well; see Cioffi-Revilla 1985a,b; Cioffi-Revilla et al. 1988). An explanation for such variations—one derived from formal theory—is to be found in the character and magnitude of the system of dynamic forces causing conflict events to occur (Cioffi-Revilla 1985a,b, 1988a).

3.5   Concept Formation

Datasets containing similar types of natural language events (e.g., crises, wars, etc.) may also be compared in terms of the scientific (operational) definition given in each dataset. To better understand the fine-structure of the conflict events recorded by the eight datasets—insofar as this is possible from their natural language definitions in the existing documentation—we shall now isolate and compare the operational definition of each event. Rather than simply repeat the text of the operational definition of the various conflict events (already reported in Sections 2.2. and 2.3, in the information field labeled **Event definition**), we shall proceed by applying a more theoretically oriented framework called the "logic success tree" modeling approach (Cioffi-Revilla 1987b, 1988a,b). Such an approach offers a useful comparative framework for analyzing the operational logic behind the occurrence (hence the name "success" tree) of political events such as crisis and war.

This section first presents some elementary ideas about logic success tree models—they are new in social science—to then apply this theoretical framework to each individual operational definition of conflict in the eight DDIR datasets. The purpose is to rigorously identify and highlight the semantic fine-structure (or operational logic) of each conflict definition, while doing so within a unified scientific framework. In addition to exposing the logic structure (or the lack of logic) of each definitional type of conflict, this approach may also be used for comparative purposes, to examine key similarities and differences across different types of international conflict events.

3.5.1   Developing Formal Comparative Models of Conflict Events Based on Logic, Sets, and Probability

A logic success tree model for the occurrence of a conflict event is based on the following considerations. First, every operational definition of conflict refers to the specification of conditions under which an event $\mathbb{E}$ (regardless of its magnitude) occurs. That is to say, given a definition of conflict (say, "1,000 fatalities per year . . .") such a definition should allow us to identify when an event from a universe of discourse U belongs or does not belong to the set of conflict events in question.

Second, every definition of conflict is axiomatically based on the *conjunction* of at least two sets of basic elements of information: *time* ($\mathbb{T}$) and *space* ($\mathbb{S}$) *conditions* for the occurrence of $\mathbb{E}$. In an intuitive sense, this is much the same as saying that conflicts—fundamentally—are events that take place at *some* point or interval in history (time condition $\mathbb{T}$), and they must also occur in the realm of interactions between *some* actors in the global system (space conditions $\mathbb{S}$). More rigorously, in the formal, mathematical sense of probability theory, the two most basic constituents of a conflict event $\mathbb{E}$ correspond to sample point-sets defined in the sample space Ω of $\mathbb{E}$ (where $U \supseteq \Omega$). The essential point—from this general theoretical perspective—is to note that the two basic elements of information about the operational occurrence of a conflict event (time and space conditions) are logically indispensable (hence the conjunction) for empirically defining a conflict event in any scientifically meaningful sense. In a probabilistic sense, the event $\mathbb{E}$ therefore occurs when a point (elemental event) within a well-defined sample point-set of time, *and* a point (another elemental event) within a well-defined sample point-set of space, co-occur.

Third, the former of these basic ingredients—time conditions T—is generally given by a historic range measured in years (e.g., the range 1495–1975 for the Levy 4A dataset). Outside of such a time range, conflict events remain undefined with respect to the set of events being included (counted) in a given dataset.[4] The second ingredient of an operational definition of

---

[4]For example, conflict events such as the Thirty Years' War, or the French-Indian wars are (natural language) conflict events *not* defined within the COW 7 dataset because their occurrence is outside the historical range of that dataset (1816–1988). In a strict sense, such events are not wars at all; at least

conflict (this is often considered to be the main part) is given by the social space discussed earlier—namely, by the specification of the types of social entities (kinds of *belligerents*) and the types of social interactions (kinds of *belligerence*) which will be stipulated to belong to the set of conflicts. [Mathematically, the sample space Ω where $\mathbb{E}$ occurs is partitioned into three subspaces, containing all possible time conditions, all possible belligerents, and all possible types (or magnitudes) of belligerence. Then $\mathbb{E}$ is simply the well-defined (and presumably non-empty) set of triplets that satisfy membership in all three subspaces of Ω.]

Finally, the qualifying types of social interactions (kinds of belligerence, or event $\mathbb{B}$) will often (not always) be specified in terms of some magnitude of conflict-related intensity, such as fatalities (e.g., 1,000 fatalities/yr in the case of COW 10-wars, or 3,200 fatalities/conflict for Richardsonian deadly quarrels).

3.5.2 Logic Success Tree Models for DDIR Conflict Events

The general approach just described may be visualized by examining the logic success tree model of conflict in Figure 3.5. (Peace and other states of the world may be analyzed using the same general theoretical framework.) The graphic model in Figure 3.5 (called a success tree) has a "resolution" of just three levels in this case, with a generic conflict event $\mathbb{E}$ at the top (this may be a crisis or a war). As indicated by the level just beneath, the occurrence of $\mathbb{E}$ (its "success," in a probabilistic sense) is governed by the conjunction of two other events (necessary conditions)—both conditions must occur for $\mathbb{E}$ to occur (hence the Boolean "AND" connector just beneath $\mathbb{E}$). Following the same general principles as before, space conditions ($\mathbb{S}$) are further specified in terms of types of actors ($\mathbb{A}$) and forms of behavior ($\mathbb{B}$) which qualify as conflict.

Because not all events and subevents that are necessary to rigorously define $\mathbb{E}$ occur in conjunction (logic Boolean "AND," which is equivalent to set intersection), a logic success tree model also uses other event connectors (Boolean "OR," "sequential [or priority] AND," "conditional AND," etc.), as shown in the upper right corner of Figure 3.5. For instance, either the occurrence of "a formal declaration of war between belligerents," or the occurrence of "over 50,000 troops involved in fighting," or the occurrence of "other important legal results" represent sufficient behavioral conditions for a

---

not in the sense of COW 7. Conversely, a dataset may very well contain some events that are not commonly known as wars in a natural language sense.

war to occur in the Wars of Modern Civilization dataset (Wright 1942: 636) of the Causes of War project. Diamond-shaped events stand for "unresolved events" (i.e., events requiring more detailed decomposition); while circles represent the most basic events—the model's "limit of resolution." Thus, the set-theoretic and logic equations for the occurrence of a generic conflict event E may be written as follows:

$$E \equiv T \cap S = T \cdot S$$

$$= T \cap (A \cap B) = T \cdot (A \cdot B),$$

where $T, A,$ and B denote temporal, actor, and behavioral conditions (i.e., the operational criteria) for the occurrence of a conflict event E, respectively.

Using this general approach, it is therefore possible to model the occurence—indeed, the very conceptual structure—of any well-defined conflict event. All eight types of interstate conflict in the DDIR datasets should meet this minimal standard, as should any other scientifically useful dataset.

For comparative purposes, Figures 3.6 through 3.13 illustrate the corresponding logic success tree models of the four crisis-type events (Figures 3.6 through 3.9) and the four war-type events (Figures 3.10 to 3.13). Although space limitations—and the main purpose of this book—do not permit extensive analytic treatment of these models here, several basic comparative aspects may be noted.

First, all eight event definitions (concepts of international conflict) yield a valid logic tree model without having to seriously modify the natural language contained in the operational definition (by either adding or deleting terms). Perhaps this new approach, which is grounded on a general theory of political events (Cioffi-Revilla 1987b, 1988a,b), can help improve the natural language definitions with a view toward making them more scientifically rigorous. A logic tree model does not necessarily guarantee the scientific status of a definition, but the inability to construct a valid model raises questions about the scientific accuracy of a definition—if a tree cannot be constructed, the defintion is probably defective. (Formally, there must be *some* way to partition the point-set E into more elemental events such that E may be unambiguously defined in terms of set and logic operations conducted on subsets of Ω.)

Second, note that only three or four levels of resolution are directly obtainable from the definitions reported in dataset sources. For analytic purposes it would be useful—indeed, theoretically important—to explore models of these conflicts with higher degree of resolution. This could be done by isolating more detailed information pertaining to actors, to behavioral events that constitute conflict, and so on. Generally speaking, the

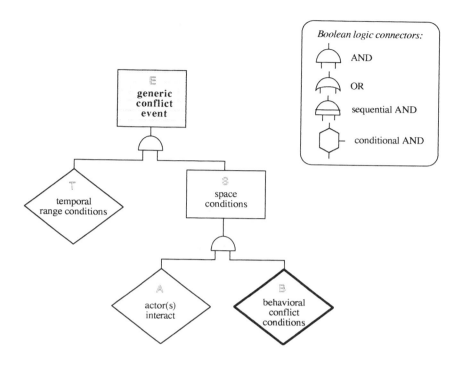

Figure 3.5 *Logic success tree model for the occurrence of a generic conflict event in a given dataset.*

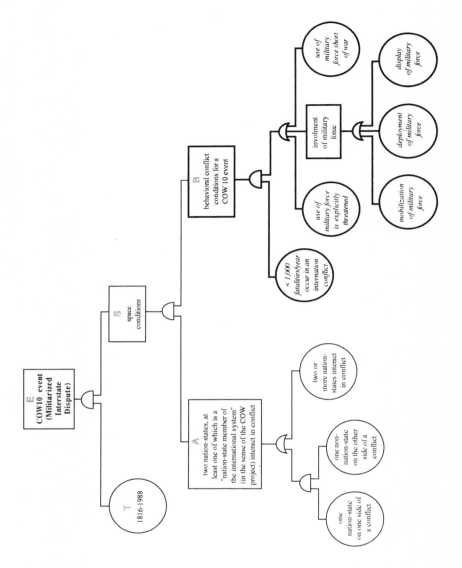

Figure 3.6 *Logic success tree for the occurrence of a Militarized Interstate Dispute event in COW 10 SS48*

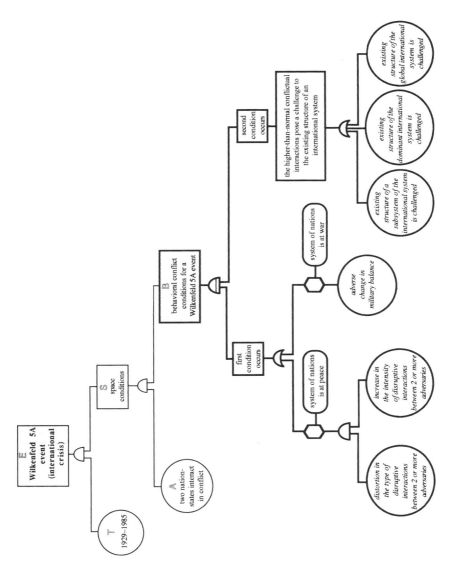

Figure 3.7 *Logic success tree for the occurrence of an International Crisis event in Wilkenfeld 5A JW1/28*

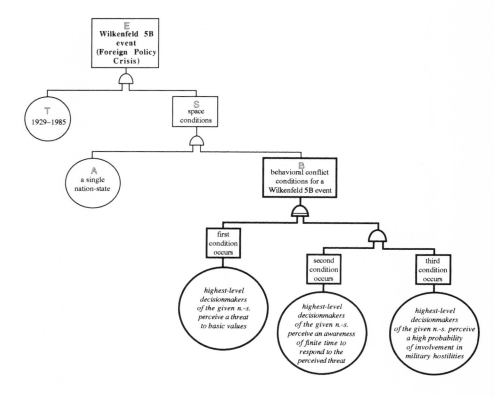

Figure 3.8 *Logic success tree for the occurrence of a Foreign Policy Crisis event in Wilkenfeld 5B JW2/28*

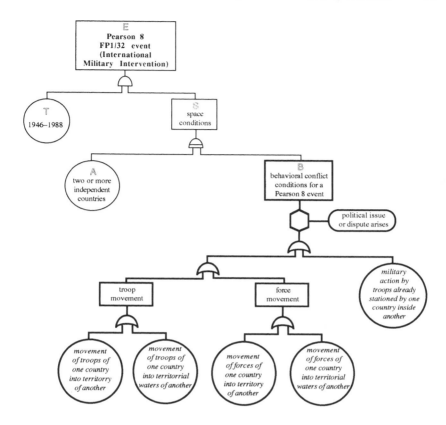

Figure 3.9 *Logic success tree for the occurrence of an International Military Intervention event in Pearson 8 FP1/32*

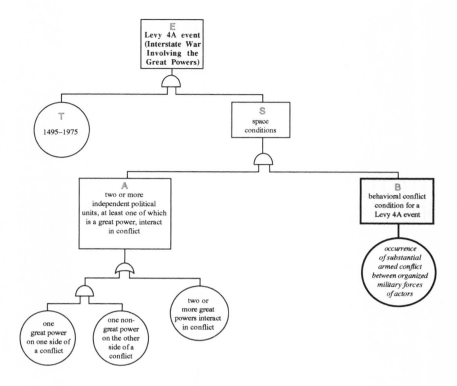

Figure 3.10 *Logic success tree for the occurrence of an Interstate War Involving Great Powers event in Levy 4A JL1/18*

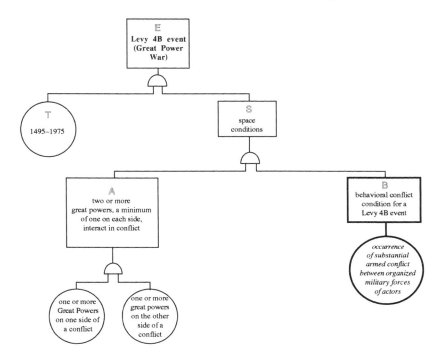

Figure 3.11 *Logic success tree for the occurrence of a Great Power War event in Levy 4B JL2/18*

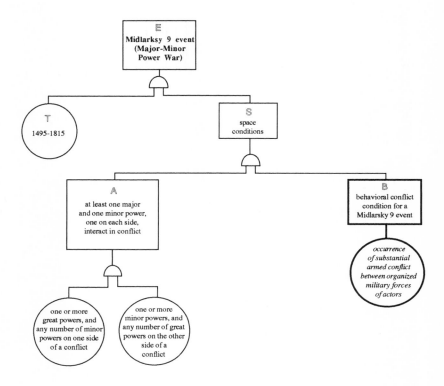

Figure 3.12 *Logic success tree for the occurrence of a Major-Minor Power War event in Midlarsky 9 ML1/54*

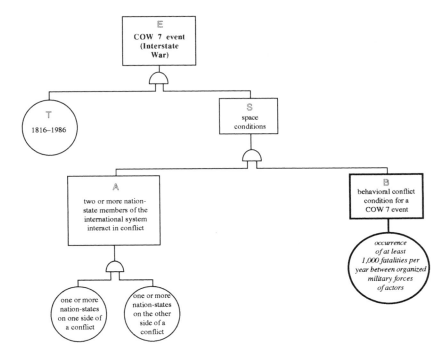

Figure 3.13 *Logic success tree for the occurrence of an Interstate War event in COW 7 SS1/5*

types of qualifying actors are better defined for severe (wars) than for potentially severe (crises) conflict events. The possible equivalence between different forms of conflict could be traced to an even greater detail if the resolution of the tree models were to be higher. Further, with greater resolution it would be possible to derive the precise correspondence between both classes of events (crises and wars). Such a result has long been expected in contemporary international relations research, and would provide foundations for a general theory of international conflict covering the full range of magnitudes.

Third, although both severe and potentially severe forms of conflict seem equally amenable to the same modeling approach, the former appears to be far more difficult to empirically detect (observe) because they generally have a much more intricate logic model (operational definition). In the epigraph at the beginning of this book, Anatol Rapoport was quite correct in referring to crises as events that can be seen only through "greater resolving power." Nonetheless, the lower resolution of severe events may be more apparent than real, because it may simply reflect greater clarity in the natural langage used to define the limiting events (e.g., "10,000 fatalities per year occur").

Future analysis—to be reported elsewhere—will derive and analyze the exact set-logic event equations for each conflict event. After algebraic simplifications (e.g., pruning, path sets, minimal path sets, etc.), the event equations pertaining to these and other conflict events could then be compared to gain a better understanding of their fine-structure and interrelationships. In particular, this new approach is clearly superior to the use of intuitive reasoning and natural language for understanding precisely what it is that each dataset is recording from history. The approach of set-logic event models can also be used to show the possible overlap or complementarity across datasets. Finally, through these and other methods it is also possible to derive canonical forms of international conflict—theoretically derived variations on essentially the same conflict events. Insights such as these may also shed valuable new light on innovative methods of conflict resolution—by identifying the prevention or occurrence of key events not easily (if at all) detectable in the raw empirical record.

3.6   Dataset Sources

Thousands of historical and social scientific sources were used for gathering the data contained in the eight DDIR interstate conflict datasets. (The profiles reported earlier in Sections 2.2 and 2.3 provide specific references for each dataset, under the information field **Event sources**.)

For comparative purposes, this section identifies only the set of core sources used by the datasets, grouped by crisis-type (potentially severe) and war-type (severe) datasets. A source core may be viewed as a "least common denominator"—it consists of those historical documentation sources used by a class of datasets. The reader is cautioned not to interpret this as meaning that the core was the only basis for gathering the information contained in these datasets. As noted earlier (Sections 2.2 and 2.3), each dataset is based on many sources in addition to the core—sometimes hundreds of other sources. In spite of this, it is useful to identify the core sources for each class of event because they reveal the genealogy of information in each and across datasets—in a genetic sense.

3.6.1 Sources for Potentially Severe International Conflicts

The four DDIR datasets containing potentially severe conflicts (crises and military interventions) are based mostly on contemporary sources (Section 2.2). Among these, the *New York Times* (and its *Index*), as well as *Keesing's Contemporary Archives*, represent core sources for coverage of conflict events after World War II. Numerous other sources supplement these two core sources in providing worldwide coverage of potentially severe conflict events.

Improved information and telecommunication technologies (e.g., automatic parsing of news wire services), supported by some as yet undiscovered system of artificial intelligence, may make the monitoring of this class of event far more practical in the future than it is today. Files of daily events data are also a possible source for this class of event (see, e.g., Eckhardt and Azar 1978).

3.6.2 Sources for Severe International Conflicts

Analysis of the information profiles reported in Section 2.3 shows that the four DDIR datasets containing severe conflicts (wars) are based on the following nine historical and social scientific core sources (in addition to hundreds of other sources specific to each dataset):

Pre-1930s. The following four, as well as other historical-statistical sources from the pre–1930s period were used by L. F. Richardson, Q. Wright, and P. A. Sorokin to compile the first social scientific datasets on war.

    [1] BODART, Gaston (1916). *Losses of Life in Modern Wars* (Oxford: Clarendon Press).

[2] DUMAS, Samuel, and K. O. VEDEL-PETERSON (1923). *Losses of Life Caused by War* (Oxford: Clarendon Press).

[3] HARBOTTLE, Thomas (1904). *Dictionary of Battles* (New York: Thomas Y. Crowell).

[4] WOODS, Frederick Adams and Alexander BALTZLY (1915). *Is War Diminishing?* (Boston: Houghton-Mifflin).

Pioneering scientific classics. The following three event collections as well as other sources were used to compile the four contemporary DDIR datasets on war.

[5] RICHARDSON, Lewis Fry ([ca. 1940s] 1960). *Statistics of Deadly Quarrels.* Quincy Wright and C. C. Lineau, eds. (Pacific Grove, Calif.: Boxwood Press).[5]

[6] SOROKIN, Pitirim A. (1937). *Social and Cultural Dynamics.* Vol. 3, *Fluctuation of Cultural Relationships, War, and Revolution* (New York: American Book Company).

[7] WRIGHT, Quincy (1942). *A Study of War* (Chicago: University of Chicago Press).

Modern behavioral classics.

[8] SINGER, J. David, and Melvin SMALL (1972). *The Wages of War, 1816–1965: A Statistical Handbook* (New York: John Wiley & Sons).

[9] SMALL, Melvin, and J. David SINGER (1982). *Resort to Arms: International and Civil Wars, 1816-1980* (Beverly Hills, Calif.: Sage Publications).

In the comparative context of the four DDIR war datasets, each of these three sets of historic and social scientific sources draws on the previous set, in the following 2-stage cumulative process:

---

[5]Lewis Fry Richardson began compiling his dataset on deadly quarrels during the early 1940s (see Richardson [1945a,b]). He died in 1953, and his dataset became public only in 1960, when Quincy Wright and Charles C. Lineau published the posthumous volume entitled *Statistics of Deadly Quarrels.*

STAGE 1:   [1], [2], [3], [4], and other sources were used by Richardson, Sorokin, and Wright to compile the first social scientific datasets, [5], [6], and [7].

STAGE 2: In turn, [5], [6], and [7], as well as other sources, were used by J. D. Singer and M. Small to compile [8] and [9], the modern behavioral classics.

Recent historical compendia. In addition to the preceding three sets of sources (pre–1930s, pioneering classics, and behavioral classics), the four DDIR war datasets, with varying emphasis, draw on the following recent historical compendia:

[10] DUPUY, R. Ernest, and Trevor N. DUPUY (1977, 1986). *The Encyclopedia of Military History from 3500 B.C. to the Present* (New York: Harper and Row).

[11] EGGENBERGER, David (1967). *An Encyclopedia of Battles* (New York: Dover).

[12] KOHN, George C. (1986). *Dictionary of Wars* (New York: Facts on File).

[13] LANGER, William L., ed. (1948, 1972). *An Encyclopedia of World History* (Boston: Houghton-Mifflin).

Aside from the sources explicitly identified in the information profile of each dataset (listed under the heading **Event source(s)**), other sources of information about these war-type events are contained in bibliographic listings separately maintained by the principal investigators. In the near future, a combined, microcomputer-based information system may become available for such a purpose.

References

ALLAN, Pierre (1979). The occurrence of international conflict in time. The Graduate Institute of International Studies, Geneva, Switzerland. Unpublished manuscript.

ALTFELD, Michael, and Bruce BUENO DE MESQUITA (1979). "Choosing sides in war," *International Studies Quarterly* **23**(1) March 1979: 87–112.

AMERICAN NATIONAL STANDARDS INSTITUTE (1977). *American National Standard for Bibliographic References* (New York: American National Standards Institute).

ANDERSON, A. D. (1956). *Structure of the Ottoman Dynasty* (Oxford, U.K.: Clarendon Press).

ANDERSON, Inguar (1956). *A History of Sweden* (New York: Praeger).

ANDERSON, M.S. (1954). "Great Britain and the Russo-Turkish War of 1768–74," *English Historical Review* **69**(270) January 1954: 39–58.

————— (1966). *The Eastern Question, 1774–1923* (London: MacMillan).

————— (1978). *Peter the Great* (London: Thames and Hudson).

ANDERSON, Roger C. (1952). *Naval Wars in the Levant, 1559–1853* (Princeton, N. J.: Princeton University Press).

ATTINÀ, Fulvio (1976). *I conflitti internazionali: Analisi e misurazione* (Milan, Italy: Franco Angeli Editore).

BAIN, R. Nisbet (1899). *The Daughter of Peter the Great* (London: Archibald Constable and Company).

BAIR, Frank E., ed. (1986). *Countries of the World and Their Leaders Yearbook 1987* (Detroit: Gale Research Company).

BANKS, Arthur S. (1971). *Cross-Polity Time Series Data* (Cambridge, Mass.: MIT Press).

BARKER, Thomas M. (1975). *The Military Intellectual and Battle* (Albany, N. Y.: State University of New York Press).

BARTON, H. Harold (1972). "Russia and the problems of Sweden and Finland, 1721–1809," *Eastern European Quarterly* **5**(4) 1972: 431–444.

BEER, Francis A. (1982). Military backgrounds of American presidential candidates. Center for International Relations, University of Colorado at Boulder. Unpublished manuscript.

———— (1983a). *Peace Against War* (San Francisco, Calif.: W. H. Freeman).

———— (1983b). United States peace-war dataset. Center for International Relations, University of Colorado at Boulder. Unpublished dataset.

———— (1983c). "Trends in American major war and peace," *Journal of Conflict Resolution* **27**(4) December 1983: 681–686.

———— (1983d). "Peace, war, and American presidents," *Political and Military Sociology* **11**(1) Spring 1983: 1–10.

———— (1984). "American major peace, war, and presidential elections," *Peace and Change* **10**(1) January 1987: 23–40.

———— (1989). Falklands/Malvinas crisis event dataset. Center for International Relations, University of Colorado at Boulder. Unpublished dataset.

BLECHMAN, Barry, and Steven S. KAPLAN (1978). *Force Without War* (Washington, D. C.: The Brookings Institution).

BOBRICK, Benson (1987). *Fearful Majesty: The Life and Reign of Ivan the Terrible* (New York: G. P. Putnam's Sons).

BODART, Gaston (1916). *Losses of Life in Modern Wars* (Oxford, U.K.: Clarendon Press).

BRECHER, Michael (1977). "Toward a theory of international crisis behavior," *International Studies Quarterly* **21**(1) 1977: 63–74.

———— (1980). *Comparative Foreign Policy Notes* **8**(2) 1980: 32–40.

———— (1984). "International crises and protracted conflicts," *International Interactions* **11**(3–4) 1984: 237–297.

———— (1989). *Crisis, Conflict and Instability* (Oxford, U.K.: Pergamon Books).

————, and Patrick JAMES (1986). *Crisis and Change in World Politics*(Boulder, Colo.: Westview Press).

————, and Jonathan WILKENFELD (1982). "Crises in world politics," *World Politics* **34**(3) April 1982: 380–417.

————, Jonathan WILKENFELD, and Stephen HILL (1987). "Threat and Violence in International Crises." In Kinhide Mushakoji, and H. Usui, eds., *Theoretical Frameworks of the Contemporary World in Transition* (Tokyo: Yushiudo Kobunshu).

————, Jonathan WILKENFELD, and Sheila MOSER (1988). *Crises in the Twentieth Century*, Vol. 1: *Handbook of Foreign Policy Crises* (New York and Oxford: Pergamon Press).

BREMER, Stuart A. (1982). "The contagiousness of coercion: The spread of serious international disputes, 1900–1976," *International Interactions* **9**(1) 1982: 29–56.

——————, and Thomas R. CUSACK (1980). "The urns of war: An application of probability theory to the genesis of war." IIVG/dp 80–128, Publication Series of the International Institute for Comparative Social Research, Wissenschaftszentrum Berlin (West Berlin, Federal Republic of Germany).

——————, J. David SINGER, and Urs LUTERBACHER (1973). "The population density and war proneness of European nations, 1816–1965," *Comparative Political Studies* **6**(3) October 1973: 329–348.

——————, et al. (1975). *The Scientific Study of War*. Learning Package Series, no. 14 (New York: Consortium for International Studies Education, for the International Studies Association).

BUENO DE MESQUITA, Bruce (1978). "Systemic polarization and the occurrence and duration of war," *Journal of Conflict Resolution* **22**(2) June 1978: 241–267.

—————— (1980). "An expected utility theory of international conflict: An exploratory study," *American Political Science Review* **74**(4) December 1980: 917–931.

—————— (1981a). *The War Trap* (New Haven, Ct.: Yale University Press).

—————— (1981b). "Risk, power distributions, and the likelihood of war," *International Studies Quarterly* **25**(4) December 1981: 541–568.

—————— (1983). "The cost of war: A rational expectations approach," *American Political Science Review* **77**(2) June 1983: 347–357.

—————— (1985). "The war trap revisited," *American Political Science Review* **79**(1) March 1985: 157–176.

——————, and Michael ALTFELD (1979). "Choosing sides in wars," *International Studies Quarterly* **23**(1) March 1979: 87–112.

——————, and David LALMAN (1986). "Reason and war," *American Political Science Review* **80**(4) December 1986: 1113–1131.

——————, and David LALMAN (1988). "Dyadic Power, Expectations, and War." In Charles Gochman, and Alan Ned Sabrosky, eds., *Prisoners of War? Nation-States in the Modern Era* (Lexington, Mass.: Lexington Books).

——————, and J. David SINGER (1973). "Alliances, capabilities, and war: A review and synthesis," *Political Science Annual* **4**, 1973: 237–280.

BUTTERWORTH, Robert L. (1976). *Managing Interstate Conflict, 1945–74: Data with Synopses* (Pittsburgh, Pa.: University Center for International Studies, University of Pittsburgh).

CANBY, Courtland (1984). *Encyclopedia of Historic Places* (New York: Facts on File).

CANNIZZO, Cynthia (1978). "Capability distribution and major power war experience, 1816–1965," *Orbis* 4 Winter 1978: 947–957.

CENTER FOR DEFENSE INFORMATION (1983). "A world at war, 1983," *Defense Monitor* 12(1) 1983.

CIOFFI-REVILLA, Claudio (1985a). "Political reliability theory and war in the international system," *American Journal of Political Science* 29(1) February 1985: 47–68.

——————— (1985b). Great power war and political reliability theory, 1495–1975. Paper presented at the 81st Annual Convention of the International Studies Association, New Orleans, August 1985.

——————— (1986). "Teoria della conflittualità internazionale," *Teoria Politica* 2(2) June 1986: 95–122.

——————— (1987a). "Crises, War, and Security Reliability." In Claudio Cioffi-Revilla, Richard L. Merritt, and Dina A. Zinnes, eds., *Communication and Interaction in Global Politics* (Beverly Hills, Calif.: Sage Publications, Inc.).

——————— (1987b). Event trees and logic models in political reliability. Paper presented at the Annual Meeting of the Midwest Political Science Association, Chicago, Illinois, 9–11 April 1987.

——————— (1988a). Fortuna Politica: A Reliability Theory of Politics. Unpublished book manuscript.

——————— (1988b). The character of war: Observational and theoretical conceptualizations. Center for International Relations, University of Colorado at Boulder. Unpublished manuscript.

——————— (1989a). "Mathematical contributions to the scientific understanding of war," *Mathematical and Computer Modeling: An International Journal* 12(4/5) 1989: 561–575.

——————— (1989b). The HYPERWAR system: A HyperCard stack of severe inter-societal conflicts from the Long-Range Analysis of War (LORANOW) project." Paper prepared for presentation at the 1989 World Conference of the International Studies Association, London, U.K., 28 March – 1 April 1989.

——————— (1989c). The international handbook of conflict datasets (IHCD). Long-Range Analysis of War (LORANOW) Project, Center for International Relations, University of Colorado at Boulder. In preparation.

———————, and Raymond DACEY (1988). "The probability of war in the *n*-crises problem: Modeling new alternatives to Wright's solution," *Synthese* 76(2) August 1988: 285–305.

———————, Stephen L. PORTNOY, Somin LO, Hugo OLIVEROS, Sa Li SU, Tracy WILSON, and K. Michelle YODER (1988). The duration of warfare in the modern great power system, 1475–1975. Long-Range Analysis of War (LORANOW) Project, Center for International Relations, University of Colorado at Boulder. Unpublished manuscript.

COLEMAN, James S. (1964). *Introduction to Mathematical Sociology* (New York: The Free Press of Glencoe).

COUGHLAN, Robert (1974). *Elizabeth and Catherine* (New York: G. P. Putnam's Sons).

CREARY, Patrick J., and Jonathan WILKENFELD (1983). Structural factors and international crisis behavior. Paper presented at the Nineteenth North American Peace Science Conference of the Peace Science Society (International), Urbana, Illinois, 7–9 November, 1983.

CREASY, E. S. (1856). *History of the Ottoman Turks* (London: Richard Bentley).

CUSACK, Thomas, and Wolf-Dieter EBERWEIN (1980). International disputes: A look at some new data. Discussion Paper dp 80–116, International Institute for Comparative Social Research, Science Center, Berlin.

CUSACK, Thomas, and Wolf-Dieter EBERWEIN (1982). "Prelude to war: Incidence, escalation and intervention in international disputes, 1900–1976," *International Interactions* 9(1) 1982: 9–28.

DIEHL, Paul (1983a). "Arms races and escalation: A closer look," *Journal of Peace Research* 20(3) 1983: 205–212.

————— (1983b). Arms races and the outbreak of war: Deterrence or provocation? Paper presented at the Annual Meetings of the Midwest Political Science Association, Chicago, 1983.

————— (1985a). "Arms races to war: Testing some empirical linkages," *Sociological Quarterly* 26(3) Fall 1985: 331–349.

————— (1985b). "Contiguity and military escalation in major power rivalries, 1816–1980," *Journal of Politics* 47(4) November 1985: 1203–1211.

DMYTRYSHYN, Basil (1977). *A History of Russia* (Englewood Cliffs, N.J.: Prentice-Hall).

DONELAN, M. D., and M. J. GRIEVE (1973). *International Disputes: Case Histories 1945–1970* (New York: St. Martin's Press).

DORAN, Charles, and Wes PARSONS (1980). "War and the cycle of relative power," *American Political Science Review* 74(4) December 1980: 947–965.

DUFFY, Christopher (1981). *Russia's Military Way to the West* (London: Routledge and Kegan Paul).

DUMAS, Samuel, and K. O. VEDEL-PETERSON (1923). *Losses of Life Caused by War* (Oxford, U.K.: Clarendon Press).

DUNCAN, George T., and Randolph M. SIVERSON (1982). "Flexibility and alliance partner choice in a multipolar system: Models and tests," *International Studies Quarterly* 26(4) December 1982: 511–538.

DUNER, Bertil (1985). *Military Intervention in Civil Wars: The 1970s* (Aldershot, U.K.: Gower).

DUPUY, R. Ernest, and Trevor N. DUPUY (1977). *The Encyclopedia of Military History from 3500 B.C. to the Present* (New York: Harper and Row).

DUPUY, R. Ernest, and Trevor N. DUPUY (1986). *The Encyclopedia of Military History from 3500 B.C. to the Present.* 2nd rev. ed. (New York: Harper and Row).

EBERWEIN, Wolf-Dieter (1981). "The quantitative study of international politics: Quantity or quality? An assessment of empirical research," *Journal of Peace Research* 18(1) 1981: 19–38.

—————, Gisela HÜBER-DICK, Wolfgang JAGODSINSKI, Hans RATTINGER, and Erich WEEDE (1976). "External and internal conflict behavior among nations, 1966–1967," *Journal of Conflict Resolution* 23(4) December 1976: 728–731.

ECKHARDT, William, and Edward E. AZAR (1978). "Major world conflicts and interventions, 1945 to 1975," *International Interactions* 5(1) 1978: 75–110.

EGGENBERGER, David (1967). *An Encyclopedia of Battles* (New York: Dover).

Encyclopedia Britannica (1910), 11th edition.

EVERSLEY, G. J. S., and Valentine CHIROL (1969). *The Turkish Empire from 1288–1924* (New York: H. Fertig).

FABER, Jan (1984). "Interaction as intermediary in the development of the European power-distribution," *Acta Politica* 19(3) July 1984: 331–341.

—————, and R. WEAVER (1984). "Participation in conferences, treaties, and warfare in the European system, 1816–1915," *Journal of Conflict Resolution* 28(3) September 1984: 522–534.

—————, Henk W. HOUWELING, and Jan G. SICCAMA (1984). "Diffusion of war: Some theoretical considerations and empirical evidence," *Journal of Peace Research* 21(3) 1984: 277–288.

FISHER, Alan W. (1970). *The Russian Annexation of the Crimea, 1772–1783* (Cambridge, U.K.: Cambridge University Press).

FISHER, Sidney N. (1959). *The Middle East: A History* (New York: Alfred A. Knopf).

GLEDITSCH, Nils Petter, and J. David SINGER (1975). "Distance and international war, 1816–1965." In *Proceedings of the IPRA Fifth General Conference*, Oslo, pp. 481–506.

GOCHMAN, Charles S. (1975). Status, Conflict, and War: The Major Powers, 1820–1970. Doctoral dissertation, Department of Political Science, University of Michigan, Ann Arbor, Michigan.

————, and Zeev MAOZ (1984). "Militarized interstate disputes, 1816–1976: Procedures, patterns, and insights," *Journal of Conflict Resolution* **28**(4) December 1984: 585–615.

————, and Zeev MAOZ (1989). "Militarized Interstate Disputes, 1816–1976." In Melvin Small, and J. David Singer, eds., pp. 44–52 *International War: An Anthology* (Chicago: Dorsey Press).

GOLDSTEIN, Joshua S. (1985). "Kondratieff waves as war cycles," *International Studies Quarterly* **29**(4) December 1985: 411–44.

———— (1987). "Long waves in war, production, prices, and wages," *International Studies Quarterly* **31**(4) December 1987: 573–600.

———— (1988). *Long Cycles: Prosperity and War in the Modern Age* (New Haven, Conn.: Yale University Press).

GREY, Ian (1973). *Boris Godunov* (London: Hodder and Stoughton).

HARBOTTLE, Thomas (1904). *Dictionary of Battles from the Earliest Date to the Present Time* (London: Sonneschein; New York: Thomas Y. Crowell).

———— (1967). *Dictionary of Battles* (New York: Thomas Y. Crowell).

———— (1971). *Dictionary of Battles*. 2nd edition. (New York: Thomas Y. Crowell).

HATTON, Ragnhild (1980). *Europe in the Age of Louis XIV* (New York: Hippocrene Books).

————, and M. S. ANDERSON (1970). *Studies in Diplomatic History* (London: Anchor Books).

HOUWELING, Henk W., and J. B. KUNÉ (1984). "Do outbreaks of war follow a Poisson process?" *Journal of Conflict Resolution* **28**(1) March 1984: 51–61.

HOUWELING, Henk W., and Jan G. SICCAMA (1985). "The epidemology of war, 1816–1980," *Journal of Conflict Resolution* **29**(4) December 1985: 641–663.

ISRAEL, Johnathan I. (1982). *The Dutch Republic and the Hispanic World, 1606–1661* (Oxford U.K.: Clarendon Press).

JAMES, Patrick (1988). *Crisis and War* (Montreal, Canada: McGill-Queen's University Press).

————, and Michael BRECHER (1988). "Stability and polarity: New paths for inquiry," *Journal of Peace Research* **25**(1) 1988: 31–42.

————, and Jonathan WILKENFELD (1984). "Structural factors in international crises," *Conflict Management and Peace Science* **7**(1): 33–53.

JOB, Brian L., and Charles W. OSTROM (1976). "An Appraisal of the Research Design and Philosophy of Science of the Correlates of War Project." In Francis W. Hoole, and Dina A. Zinnes, eds., *Quantitative International Politics: An Appraisal* (New York: Praeger).

JONES, Archer (1987). *The Art of War in the Western World* (Chicago: University of Illinois Press).

JONES, Daniel (1987). The onset of minor-power disputes, 1945–1985. Paper presented at the Annual Meetings of the Midwest Political Science Association, Chicago, 10 April 1987.

KEMENY, John G., and J. Laurie SNELL (1962). *Mathematical Models in the Social Sciences* (Cambridge, Mass.: The MIT Press).

KENDE, Istvan (1971). "Wars of ten years: 1967–1976," *Journal of Peace Research* **15**(3) 1978: 227–241.

———— (1978). "Twenty-five years of local wars," *Journal of Peace Research* **8**(1) 1971: 5–22.

KOHN, George C. (1986). *Dictionary of Wars* (New York: Facts on File).

LANGER, W. L., ed. (1948). *An Encyclopedia of World History* (Boston: Houghton-Mifflin).

————, ed. (1972). *An Encyclopedia of World History,* 5th ed., rev. (Boston: Houghton-Mifflin).

LANGER, Herbert (1980). *Thirty Years War* (New York: Hippocrene Books).

LENG, Russell J., and Charles GOCHMAN (1982). "Dangerous disputes: A study of conflict behavior and war," *American Journal of Political Science* **26**(4) November 1982: 664–687.

LENG, Russell J., and Robert A. GOODSELL (1974). "Behavioral indicators of war proneness in bilateral conflicts." In Patrick McGowan, ed., *Sage International Yearbook of Foreign Policy Studies* **2**, 1974: 191–226.

LENG, Russell J., and Hugh WHEELER (1979). "Influence strategies, success and war," *Journal of Conflict Resolution* **23**(4) December 1979: 655–284.

LEVY, Jack S. (1981). "Alliance formation and war behavior: An analysis of the great powers, 1495–1975," *Journal of Conflict Resolution* **25**(4) December 1981: 581–614.

————— (1982a). "The contagion of great power war behavior," *American Journal of Political Science* **26**(3) August 1982: 562–584.

————— (1982b). "Historical trends in great power war, 1495–1975," *International Studies Quarterly* **26**(2) June 1982: 278–301.

————— (1983a). *War in the Modern Great Power System, 1495–1975* (Lexington, Ky.: University Press of Kentucky).

————— (1983b). "World systems analysis: A great power perspective." In William R. Thompson, ed., *World System Analysis: Competing Approaches* (Beverly Hills, Calif.: Sage Publications).

————— (1984a). "The offensive/defensive balance of military technology: A theoretical and historical analysis," *International Studies Quarterly* **28**(2) 1984: 219–238.

————— (1984b). "Size and stability in the modern great power system," *International Interactions* **10**(3–4): 76–99.

————— (1985a). "Theories of general war," *World Politics* **37**(3) April 1985: 344–374.

————— (1985b). "The Polarity of the System and International Stability: An Empirical Analysis." In Alan Ned Sabrosky, ed., *Polarity and War: The Changing Structure of International Conflict*, pp. 41–66 (Boulder, Colo.: Westview Press).

————— (1988a). "Analytic problems in the definition of wars," *International Interactions* **14**(2) 1988: 181–186.

————— (1988b). "Great power wars," *DDIR-UPDATE* **3**(1) August 1988: 2.

————— (1989). Great power wars dataset: DDIR bibliography. January 1989. Unpublished manuscript.

—————, and T. Clifton MORGAN (1984). "The frequency and seriousness of war: An inverse relationship?" *Journal of Conflict Resolution* **28**(4) December 1984: 731–749.

—————, and T. Clifton MORGAN (1986a). "The war-weariness hypothesis: An empirical test," *American Political Science Review* **30**(1) February 1986: 26–49.

—————, and T. Clifton MORGAN (1986b). "The Structure of the International System and the Frequency and Seriousness of War." In Margaret P. Karns, ed., *Persistent Patterns and Emergent Structures in a Waning Century*, pp. 75–98 (New York: Praeger).

LONGWORTH, Philip (1984). *Alexis Tzar of All the Russians* (London: Secker and Warburg).

LORD, Robert H. (1915). *The Second Partition of Poland* (Cambridge, Mass.: Harvard University Press).

LUARD, Evan, ed. (1970). *The International Regulation of Frontier Disputes* (London: Thames and Hudson).

MALAND, David (1980). *Europe at War* (Totowa, N.J.: Rowman and Littlefield).

MAOZ, Zeev (1982). *Paths to Conflict: International Dispute Initiation, 1816–1976* (Boulder, Colo.: Westview Press).

————— (1983a). "Resolve, capabilities, and the outcome of interstate disputes, 1816–1976," *Journal of Conflict Resolution* 27(2) June 1983: 195–229.

————— (1983b). "A behavioral model of dispute escalation: The major powers 1816–1976," *International Interactions* 10(3–4) 1983: 373–399.

MCKAY, Derek (1981). *Prince Eugene of Savoy* (London: Routledge and Kegan Paul).

—————, and H. M. SCOTT (1983). *The Rise of the Great Powers, 1648–1815* (London: Longman).

MCNEIL, William H. (1964). *Europe's Steppe Frontier* (Chicago: University of Chicago Press).

MERRIMAN, Roger Bigelow (1944). *Suleiman the Magnificent* (Cambridge, Mass.: Harvard University Press).

————— (1962). *The Rise of the Spanish Empire in the Old World and the New* (New York: Cooper Square Publishers).

MERRITT, Richard L., and Dina A. ZINNES (1986). Data development in international research. Merriam Laboratory for Analytical Political Research, University of Illinois at Urbana-Champaign. Unpublished manuscript.

MIDLARSKY, Manus I. (1974). "Power, uncertainty, and the onset of international violence," *Journal of Conflict Resolution* 18(3) September 1974: 395–431.

————— (1975). *On War: Political Violence in the International System* (New York: Free Press).

————— (1986a). "A hierarchical equilibrium theory of systemic war," *International Studies Quarterly* 30(2) 1986: 77–105.

————— (1986b). *The Disintegration of Political Systems: War and Revolution in Comparative Perspective* (Columbia, S.C.: University of South Carolina Press).

————— (1988a). "Theoretical foundations for the collection of major power-minor power war data," *International Interactions* 14(2) 1988: 187–190.

————— (1988b). "Major-minor powers," *DDIR-UPDATE,* 3(1) August 1988: 2–3.

————— (1988c). *The Onset of World War* (Boston: Unwin Hyman).

—————, and Kun Y. PARK (1988). Documentation of DDIR Project: Minor power-Minor power wars. Center for International Relations,

University of Colorado at Boulder. Unpublished codebook manuscript. September 1988.

MIHALKA, Michael (1976). "Hostilities in the European state system, 1816–1970," *Peace Science Society (International) Papers* **26**, 1976: 100–116.

MITCHELL, B. R. (1978). *European Historical Statistics, 1740–1970* (New York: Columbia University Press).

MODELSKI, George, and Patrick M. MORGAN (1985). "Understanding global war," *Journal of Conflict Resolution* **29**(3) September 1985: 391–417.

MONTROLL, Elliot, and Wade W. BADGER, eds. (1974). *Introduction to Quantitative Aspects of Social Phenomena* (New York: Gordon and Breach Science Publishers).

MORGAN, T. Clifton, and Jack S. LEVY (1986). "The Structure of the International System and the Frequency and Seriousness of War." In Margaret P. Karns, ed., *Persistent Patterns and Emergent Structures in a Waning Century*, pp. 75–98 (New York: Praeger).

——————— (1989). "Base Stealers and Power Hitters: A Nation-State Level Analysis of the Frequency and Seriousness of War." In Charles S. Gochman and Alan Ned Sabrosky, eds., *Prisoners of War* (Lexington, Mass.: Lexington Books).

MOST, Benjamin J., and Harvey STARR (1980). "Diffusion, reinforcement, geopolitics, and the spread of war," *American Political Science Review* **74**(4) December 1980: 932–946.

MOYAL, J. (1949) "The distribution of wars in time," *Journal of the Royal Statistical Society* (Series A) **112**(IV) 1949: 446–469.

MURRAY, John J. (1969). *George I, the Baltic and the Whig Split of 1717* (Chicago: University of Chicago Press).

NAROLL, Raoul, Vern L. BULLOULEH, and Frada NAROLL (1974). *Military Deterrence in History* (Albany, N.Y.: State University Press of New York).

NORTHEDGE, F. S., and M. D. DONELAN (1971). *International Disputes: The Political Aspects* (London: Europa Publications).

PEARSON, Frederick S. (1973). [Dataset on foreign military interventions for the period 1948–1967] *Occasional Paper no. 732*, Center for International Studies, University of Missouri, St. Louis, Missouri.

——————— (1974). "Foreign military intervention and domestic disputes," *International Studies Quarterly* **18**(3) September 1974: 259–290.

——————— (1984). "Geographic proximity and foreign military interventions," *Journal of Conflict Resolution* **18**(3) September 1984: 432–460.

——————— (1987). International military interventions: Identification and classification. Paper presented at the Annual Convention of the International Studies Association, Washington, D.C., April 1987.

——————— (1988). "Interventions," *DDIR-UPDATE* 3(1) August 1988: 3–4.

PITCHER, Donald E. (1985). *Historical Geography of the Ottoman Empire* (New York: Macmillan).

POLISENSKY, Josef V. (1970). *The Thirty Years War* (London: B. T. Batsford).

RAPOPORT, Anatol (1983). *Mathematical Models in the Social and Behavioral Sciences* (New York: John Wiley and Sons).

RAY, James Lee (1974). "Status inconsistency and war involvement in Europe, 1816–1970," *Peace Science Society (International) Papers* **23**, 1974: 69–80.

——————— , and Charles GOCHMAN (1979). "Structural disparities in Latin America and Europe, 1950–1970," *Journal of Peace Research* **16**(3) 1979: 231–254.

RICHARDSON, Lewis Fry (1941). "Frequency of occurrence of wars and other fatal quarrels," *Nature* **148**, 15 November 1941: 598.

——————— (1945a). "Distribution of wars in time," *Nature* **155**(3942) 19 May 1945: 610.

——————— (1945b). "The distribution of wars in time," *Journal of the Royal Statistical Society* **107**(III–IV) 1945: 242–250.

——————— (1952). "Is it possible to prove any general statements about historical fact?" *British Journal of Sociology* **3**(1) March 1952: 77–84.

——————— (1960). *Statistics of Deadly Quarrels* (Pacific Grove, Calif.: Boxwood Press). Posthumously compiled by Charles C. Lineau, and Quincy Wright, eds.

ROBERTS, Michael (1968). *The Early Vasas: A History of Sweden, 1523–1611* (Cambridge, U.K.: Cambridge University Press).

ROIDER, Karl A., Jr. (1972). *The Reluctant Ally: Austria's Policy in the Austro-Turkish War, 1737–1739* (Baton Rouge, La.: Louisiana State University Press).

RUSSELL, J. C., ed. (1958). *Transactions of the American Philosophical Society* **48**(3). Philadelphia: American Philosophical Society.

SABROSKY, Alan Ned (1976). Why Wide Wars? Capability Distribution, Alliance Aggregation, and the Expansion of Interstate War, 1816–1965. Doctoral dissertation, Department of Political Science, University of Michigan, Ann Arbor, Michigan.

SCHAMA, Simon (1987). *The Embarrassment of Riches* (New York: Alfred A. Knopf).

SCHMID, Alex P., and Ellen BERENDS (1985). Soviet military interventions since 1945. Research Report no. 17, Center for the Study of Social Conflicts, State University of Leiden, Netherlands.

SINGER, J. David (1972). "The Correlates of War Project: Interim report and rationale," *World Politics* **24**(2) January 1972: 243–270.

————— (1976). "The Correlates of War Project: Continuity, Diversity, and Convergence." In Frank Hoole, and Dina A. Zinnes, eds., *Quantitative International Politics: An Appraisal*, pp. 21–66 (New York: Praeger).

————— (1979a). The management of serious international disputes. Paper presented at the XIth World Congress of the International Political Science Association, Moscow, U.S.S.R., 12–18 August, 1979.

————— (1980). "Conflict Research, Political Action, and Epistemology." In Ted Robert Gurr, ed., *Handbook of Conflict Theory and Research*, pp. 140–149 (New York: Free Press).

————— (1981). "Accounting for international war: The state of the discipline," *Journal of Peace Research* **18**(1) 1981: 1–18.

————— (1982). "Confrontational behavior and escalation to war, 1816–1950: A research plan," *Journal of Peace Research* **19**(1) 1982: 37–48.

————— (1989). Letter to Lynne C. Rienner [peer review of this book ms.]. 27 June 1989.

—————, ed. (1979b). *Correlates of War II: Testing Some Realpolitik Models* (New York: Free Press).

—————, and ASSOCIATES (1979). *Explaining War: Selected Papers from the Correlates of War Project* (Beverly Hills, Calif.: Sage Publications).

—————, and Sandra BOUXSEIN (1975). "Structural clarity and international war: Some tentative findings." In Murray, ed., *Interdisciplinary Aspects of General Systems Theory*, pp. 126–135.

—————, Stuart A. BREMER, and John STUCKEY (1972). "Capability Distribution, Uncertainty, and Major Power War, 1820–1965." In Bruce M. Russett, ed., *Peace, War, and Numbers*, pp. 19–48 (Beverly Hills, Calif.: Sage Publications).

—————, and Thomas CUSACK (1981). "Periodicity, Inexorability, and Steersmanship in Major Power War." In Richard L. Merritt, and Bruce M. Russett, eds., *From National Development to Global Community*, pp. 404–422 (London: Allen and Unwin).

—————, and Melvin SMALL (1966). "National alliance commitments and war involvement, 1815–1945," *Peace Research Society (International) Papers* **5**, 1966: 109–140.

—————, and Melvin SMALL (1968). "Alliance Aggregation and the Onset of War, 1815–1945." In J. David Singer, ed., *Quantitative International Politics: Insights and Evidence*, pp. 247–286 (New York: Free Press).

—————, and Melvin SMALL (1970). "Patterns in international warfare, 1816–1965," *American Academy of Political and Social Science* **391** (3) September 1970: 145–155.

—————, and Melvin SMALL (1972). *The Wages of War, 1816–1965: A Statistical Handbook* (New York: John Wiley and Sons).

—————, and Melvin SMALL (1974). "Foreign policy indicators: Predictors of war in history and in the State of the World Message," *Policy Sciences* **5**(3) September 1974: 271–296.

—————, and Melvin SMALL (1984). *The Wages of War, 1816–1980: Augmented with Disputes and Civil War Data. Part 3: Interstate Disputes.* ICPSR Codebook of ICPSR file no. 9044 (Ann Arbor, Mich.: Inter-University Consortium for Political and Social Research).

—————, and Richard J. STOLL (1984). *Quantitative Indicators in World Politics: Timely Assurance and Early Warning* (New York: Praeger).

—————, and Michael D. WALLACE (1970). "Inter–governmental organization and the preservation of peace, 1816–1965: Some bivariate relationships," *International Organization* **24**(3) Summer 1970: 520–547.

—————, and Michael D. WALLACE (1979). *To Augur Well: Early Warning Indicators in World Politics* (Beverly Hills, Calif.: Sage Publications).

SIVERSON, Randolph M., and Joel KING (1980). "Attributes of national alliance membership and war participation," *American Journal of Political Science* **24**(1) February 1980: 1–15.

SIVERSON, Randolph M., and Michael SULLIVAN (1983). "The distribution of power and the onset of war," *Journal of Conflict Resolution* **27**(3): 473–494.

SIVERSON, Randolph M., and Michael R. TENNEFOSS (1982). "Interstate Conflicts: 1815–1965," *International Interactions* **9**(2) July 1982: 147–178.

SKJELSBAEK, Kjell (1972). "Shared Memberships in Intergovernmental Organizations and Dyadic War, 1865–1964." In E. H. Fedder, ed., *The United Nations: Problems and Prospects*, pp. 31–61 (St. Louis, Mo.: Center for International Studies).

SMALL, Melvin (1976). "The applicability of quantitative international politics to diplomatic history," *The Historian* 38(1) February 1976: 281–304.

——————— (1978). "Does size make a difference? The Martial and Diplomatic Experience of Major and Other Powers, 1816–1977." In Amstrup and Faurby, eds., *Studier i Dansk Udenrigspolitik* (Aarhus, Denmark: Forlaget Politica).

———————, and J. David SINGER (1970). "Patterns in international warfare, 1816–1965," *Annals of the American Academy of Political and Social Science* 391, September 1970: 145–155.

———————, and J. David SINGER (1976). "The war proneness of democratic regimes, 1816–1965," *Jerusalem Journal of International Relations* 1(4) Summer 1976: 49–69.

———————, and J. David SINGER (1979). "Conflict in the International System, 1816–1977: Historical Trends and Policy Futures." In Charles W. Kegley, and Patrick J. McGowan, eds., *Challenges to America: United States Foreign Policy in the 1980s*, pp. 89–115 (Beverly Hills, Calif.: Sage Publications).

———————, and J. David SINGER (1982). *Resort to Arms: International and Civil Wars, 1816–1980* (Beverly Hills, Calif.: Sage Publications).

———————, and J. David SINGER, eds. (1989). *International War: An Anthology* (Chicago: Dorsey).

SOREL, Albert (1898). *The Eastern Question in the Eighteenth Century* (London: Methuen and Company).

SOROKIN, Pitirim A. (1937). *Social and Cultural Dynamics, Vol. 3, Fluctuation of Social Relationships, War, and Revolution* (New York: American Book Company).

SPIELMAN, John P. (1977). *Leopold I of Austria* (London: Thames and Hudson).

STARR, Harvey (1987). "International data as a national resource," *DDIR-Update* 1(3) February 1987: Appendix, pp. 5–6

Statesman's Year-book: Statistical and Historical Annual of the States of the World for the Year 1914 (London: Macmillan). 1914.

STEVENS, S. S. (1951). "Mathematics, Measurement, and Psychophysics." In *Handbook of Experimental Psychology*, pp. 1–49 (New York: John Wiley and Sons).

STOLL, Richard J. (1977). An attempt to scale major power disputes, 1816–1965: The use of a method to detect development processes. Paper presented at the Annual Convention of the International Studies Association, St. Louis, Missouri, 1977.

——————— (1982). "Major power interstate conflict in the post-World War II era: An increase, a decrease, or no change?," *Western Political Quarterly* **35**(4) December 1982: 587–605.

——————— (1983). "Nations at the brink: A computer application of governmental behavior during serious disputes," *Simulation and Games* **14**(2) June 1982: 179–200.

——————— (1984a). "Bloc concentration and dispute escalation among the major powers, 1830–1965," *Social Science Quarterly* **65**(1) March 1984: 48–59.

——————— (1984b). "From fire to frying pan: The impact of major power war involvement on major power dispute involvement, 1816–1976," *Conflict Management and Peace Science* **7**(2) Spring 1984: 71–82.

———————, and Michael CHAMPION (1977). Predicting the escalation of serious disputes to international war: Some preliminary findings. Paper presented at the North American Meeting of the Peace Science Society (International), Philadelphia, 1977.

———————, and Michael CHAMPION (1985). "Capability Concentration, Alliance Bonding, and Conflict Among the Major Powers." In Alan Ned Sabrosky, ed., *Polarity and War: The Structure of International Conflict*, pp. 67–94 (Boulder, Colo.: Westview Press).

SYMCOX (1983). *Victor Amadeus II: Absolutism in the Sovoyard State 1675–1730* (Berkeley, Calif.: University of California Press).

TAPIE, Victor L. (1971). *Rise and Fall of the Hapsburg Monarchy* (New York: Praeger).

THOMPSON, William R. (1982). "Phases of the business cycle and the outbreak of war," *International Studies Quarterly* **26**(2) June 1982: 301–311.

——————— (1985). "Cycles of General, Hegemonic, and Global War." In Urs Luterbacher, and Michael D. Ward, eds., *Dynamic Models of International Conflict*, pp. 462–488 (Boulder, Colo.: Lynne Rienner Publishers).

———————, Robert DUVAL, and Ahmed DIA (1979). "Wars, alliances, and military expenditure," *Journal of Conflict Resolution* **23**(4) December 1979: 629–654.

TILLEMA, Herbert K. (1973). *Appeal to Force: American Military Intervention in the Era of Containment* (New York: Thomas Y. Crowell Company).

——————— (1986). Regional patterns in international military intervention: State's orientation toward the use of force, 1946–1983. Paper presented at the Annual Convention of the International Studies Association, Anaheim, Calif., 25–29 March 1986.

——————, and John R. VAN WINGEN (1982). "Law and power in military intervention: Major states after World War II," *International Studies Quarterly* **26**(2) June 1982: 220–250.

VAN WINGEN, John R., and Herbert K. TILLEMA (1980). "British military intervention after World War II: Militance in a second-rank order," *Journal of Peace Research* **17**(4) 1980: 291–303.

VASQUEZ, John A. (1976). "Statistical findings in international politics: A data-based assessment," *International Studies Quarterly* **20**(2) June 1976: 171–218.

VAYRYNEN, Raimo (1983). "Economic cycles, power transitions, political management and wars between major powers," *International Studies Quarterly* **27**(4) December 1983: 389–418.

WALISZEWSKI, K. (1898). *Peter the Great* (London: William Heinemann).

WALLACE, Michael D. (1971). "Power, status, and international war," *Journal of Peace Research* **1**(1) 1971: 23–35.

——————— (1972). "Status, Formal Organization, and Arms Levels as Factors Leading to the Onset of War, 1820–1964." In Bruce M. Russett, ed., *Peace, War, and Numbers*, pp. 49–69 (Beverly Hills, Calif.: Sage Publications).

——————— (1973a). *War and Rank Among Nations* (Lexington, Mass.: Lexington Books).

——————— (1973b). "Alliance polarization, cross-cutting, and international war, 1815–1964: A measurement procedure and some preliminary evidence," *Journal of Conflict Resolution* **17**(4) December 1973: 575–604.

——————— (1979). "Arms races and escalation: Some new evidence," *Journal of Conflict Resolution* **23**(1) March 1979: 3–16.

——————— (1981). "Old nails in new coffins: The *parabelum* hypothesis revisited," *Journal of Peace Research* **18**(1) 1981: 91–96.

——————— (1982). "Armaments and escalation," *International Studies Quarterly* **26**(1) March 1982: 37–56.

WALLENSTEEN, Peter (1981). "Incompatibility, confrontation, and war: Four models and three historical systems, 1816–1976," *Journal of Peace Research* **18**(1) 1981: 57–90.

WAYMAN, Frank (1982). War and power transitions during enduring rivalries. Paper presented at the 1982 Meeting of the Institute for the Study of Conflict Theory and International Security, University of Illinois at Champaign-Urbana, April 1982.

——————— (1984). "Bipolarity and war: The role of capability concentration and alliance patterns among major powers," *Journal of Peace Research* **21**(1) 1984: 61–78.

——————, J. David SINGER, and Gary GOERTZ (1983). "Capabilities, allocations, and success in militarized disputes and wars, 1816–1976," *International Studies Quarterly* **27**(4) December 1983: 497–516.

WEEDE, Erich (1970). "Conflict behavior of nation states," *Journal of Peace Research* **7**(3) 1970: 229–237.

—————— (1974). "Status inconsistency and war involvement in Europe, 1816–1970," *Peace Science Society (International) Papers* **23**: 69–80.

—————— (1981). "Preventing war by nuclear deterrence or by detente," *Conflict Management and Peace Science* **6**(1) 1981: 1–18.

—————— (1984). "Democracy and war involvement," *Journal of Conflict Resolution* **28**(4) December 1984: 649–664.

WESTING, Arthur H. (1982). "War as a human endeavor: The high-fatality wars of the twentieth century," *Journal of Peace Research* **19**(3) 1982: 261–270.

WHEELER, Hugh (1975). "Effects of war on industrial growth," *Society* **12**(4) May/June 1975: 48–52.

WILKENFELD, Jonathan (1988). "International crisis behavior," *DDIR-UPDATE* **3**(1) August 1988: 4–5.

——————, and Michael BRECHER (1982). "Superpower Crisis Management Behavior." In Charles W. Kegley and Patrick J. McGowan (eds.), *Foreign Policy: US/USSR* (Beverly Hills, Calif.: Sage Publications).

——————, and Michael BRECHER (1984). "International crises, 1945–1975: The U.N. dimension," *International Studies Quarterly* **28**(1) March 1984: 45–67.

——————, Michael BRECHER, and Sheila MOSER (1988). *Crises in the Twentieth Century, Vol. 2: Handbook of Foreign Policy Crises.* (New York and Oxford: Pergamon Press).

WILLIAMS, Neville (1968). *Chronology of the Modern World: 1763 to the Present Time* (New York: David McKay).

—————— (1969). *Chronology of the Expanding World: 1492–1762* (New York: David McKay).

WILLIAMSON, Paul R., John WARNER, and Stephen A. HOPKINS (1988). A model of international dispute onsets with preliminary application to the impact of nuclear weapons. Correlates of War (COW) Project, University of Michigan at Ann Arbor. Unpublished manuscript.

WITTEK, Paul (1963). *Rise of the Ottoman Empire* (London: Royal Asiatic Society).

WITTMAN, Donald (1979). "How a war ends," *Journal of Conflict Resolution* **23**(4) December 1979: 743–765.

WOODS, Frederick Adams, and Alexander BALTZLY (1915). *Is War Diminishing?* (Boston: Houghton-Mifflin).

WRIGHT, Quincy (1942). *A Study of War* (Chicago: The University of Chicago Press).

ZACHER, Mark W. (1979). *International Conflicts and Collective Security, 1946–1977* (New York: Praeger).

About the Author

CLAUDIO CIOFFI-REVILLA is Associate Professor of Political Science, and director of the Center for International Relations, at the University of Colorado at Boulder. His current research program, the Long-Range Analysis of War (LORANOW) Project, aims at developing mathematical models and a new dataset of war and peace processes from the antiquity to the present. He is co-director of the Scuola Internazionale di Metodologia e Modelli Matematici Applicati alle Scienze Sociali, Gorizia (Trieste). Professor Cioffi holds degrees in political science (international relations) from the Facoltà di Scienze Politiche Cesare Alfieri of the Università degli Studi di Firenze, Italy (1977), and from the State University of New York at Buffalo (1979). An author of numerous publications on the application of mathematical models (probability theory) to the study of war and peace, Professor Cioffi is an elected member of the International Medici Academy, and an Anatol Rapoport Fellow of the Canadian Peace Research Institute-Dundas. In 1988, he received the Best Paper Award of the Symposium on Systems Engineering and Peace Research of the Austrian Society for Cybernetics. His wife Jean is an accomplished performer, conductor, and teacher of early music (medieval, Renaissance and early baroque).